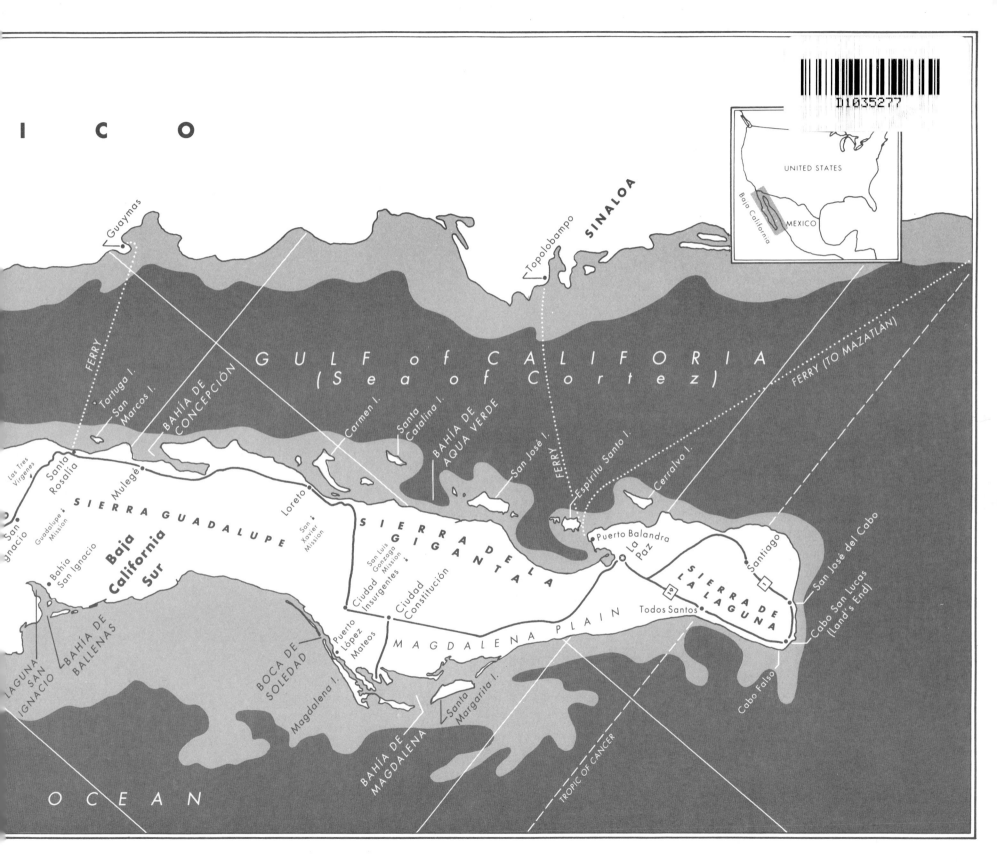

¡baja!

photographs by **Terrence Moore**
text by **Doug Peacock**
introduction by **Peter Matthiessen**

¡baja!

Bulfinch Press   Little, Brown and Company   Boston Toronto London

first edition

Excerpts on the following pages were taken from:
Pages 41, 102, 125, 132: Edward Abbey, *Desert Solitaire*.
Pages 129, 155: Joseph Wood Krutch, *The Forgotten Peninsula*.
Pages 80, 119, 175: John Steinbeck, *The Log from the Sea of Cortez*.
Pages 54–55, 65, 66, 126: John C. Van Dyke, *The Desert*.
Pages 70, 156: Ann Zwinger, *A Desert Country Near the Sea:
A Natural History of the Cape Region of Baja California*.

Photographs on the following pages courtesy of:
Pages 23, 141(left), 162, 166–67(center): Suzi Moore
Pages 163, 166(left): C. Allan Morgan

Library of Congress Cataloging-in-Publication Data

Moore, Terrence.
  Baja!/photographs by Terrence Moore; text by Doug Peacock, with
an introduction by Peter Matthiessen. — 1st ed.
    p.   cm.
  ISBN 0-8212-1803-4
  1. Baja California (Mexico) — Description and travel.   2. Baja
California (Mexico) — Description and travel — Views.   I. Peacock,
Doug.   II. Title.
F1246.M76   1991
972'.2 — dc20   91-10666

Bulfinch Press is an imprint and trademark of Little, Brown and Company (Inc.)

Published simultaneously in Canada by Little, Brown & Company (Canada) Limited

PRINTED IN SINGAPORE

Frontispiece: A late evening view from Cholluda Island across the Gulf of California to Tiburón Island, looking through a forest of cardon and pitahaya cactus.

contents

author's note: land of the giants

During the lunar year of 1989, the year of the rat, I had occasion to spend two hundred nights camping out. I know the exact number because I had to add up the days in order to figure out my income tax for 1989 — probably the last year I will slide by on the zero tax I have paid all my life. But times change — sometimes radically — as they did this past year.

My two hundred nights were spent sleeping under the stars, in my tent along rivers in the Yukon and Alaska, or in the dunes of southern Baja, the fog rolling in off the Pacific. When the year began, I found myself on Tiburón Island in the Sea of Cortez with Yvon Chouinard and other friends, taking a nervous break from closely watching the declining health of my old friend Ed Abbey. By the end of the lunar year, I was back in Mexico with Yvon Chouinard again, this time joined by Peter Matthiessen and photographer Terry Moore, in south-central Baja. The purpose of the trip was to collaborate on a book — a book Ed Abbey had intended to do before his death on March 16, 1989.

Ed's passing was the indirect cause of my camping out for seven months. Although his death was not unexpected and the man was well prepared for his departure, the dying was hard on his family and several of his closest friends. By the time I returned from the Sea of Cortez to Tucson to see Ed into the hospital the last time for the high-tech medicine he hated, then out to die on the desert where he suddenly got better ("Sometimes the magic doesn't work," he said), two more days and nights to the end, and then back out into the desert hills we both loved to be buried under a pile of black rocks, the deathwatch had taken its toll on this knot of friends and family members. Then there were the memorials and wakes (hard on the health of the living). When it was all over, I found that I myself had walked a bit too far into death and it took me a good while to come back; I had lost a certain zest for life.

At the same time, the Federal Bureau of Investigation — having grown bold and restless in the wake of *Valdez* and the death of Ed Abbey — was busting "radical environmentalists" throughout the American West. Elsewhere, the effluvium of oil spills was washing up on thousands of miles of wild beaches, and the entire natural world seemed to be burning.

I wanted to put out the fire, of course, but sometimes it's hard to know exactly what to do. The "Shiny Shoe" boys were also knocking on my door, terrifying the gardener hired to water our trees, a fourteen-year-old girl who will not speak of her experience with the FBI to this day. Additionally, my health was going all to hell, mostly the result of too many decades of hard living and repeated bouts of giardiasis and other parasitic

Silhouettes of the Central Desert with early morning fog.

waterborne diseases resulting from drinking untreated water in the Brooks Range, the Sierra Madre, and several of the wildest ranges of Canada and southern Alaska simply because I refused to accept the proposition that all the water on earth was poisoned (it seems I may have been wrong in this).

My reaction to all this turmoil was to go camp out some more; it's cheaper than consulting professionals and usually works for me. Abbey's editor had asked Peter Matthiessen and me to take over Ed's part of the Baja book. I loved this part of the desert and wanted to arm those who would visit this delicate land with an ethic aimed at preserving its fragile beauty. Putting my energy and focus into such a project seemed as constructive a way as anything I could come up with to take on the world environmental crisis and the current disarray my life was in. Change or die, they say. So I hit the backroads of Mexico again. Years ago, my friend Ed (cribbing from Kazantzakis) had pointed out that the warrior's strength is rooted in the joy of loving the earth. In late 1989, I again found myself on the Baja Peninsula, this time researching the book — a work I initially envisioned as a cookbook of sorts, encompassing the indigenous animals and native plants, a kind of gluttonous ethnobotany — and inching my pickup over the granite trails of the

ten-thousand-foot-high San Pedro Mártir, where grizzlies once roamed. I drove through groves of live oaks and down into washes where chiletepin bushes grew under wolfberry thickets. Below was the Pacific Ocean — beaches loaded with Pismo, Chione, and Dosinia clams — where I intended to dig shellfish for dinner.

Later, I ran into serious doubts. Not the least of these was the question of who the hell was I, this tourist, tethered to his gashog pickup truck driving the roads, who went looking for the last of the Paipáis but couldn't find any; who could count on one hand his close friends among the native inhabitants of northwestern Mexico?

You have to get by this kind of thinking if you're going to write a book, though it did become clear my ambitions for the book on Baja and the gulf would be limited. The land is so big and any one life passes quickly over so little of it. The only places I felt I knew were the wilder ones; I cared little for hotels, four-star or otherwise. The few resort places I remember tend to be the ones that burned me for a few thousand extra pesos for a boat ride. There is a disproportionate amount of material describing the interface of land and sea, shortchanging the interior desert. The entire cape region, the most popular tourist area, is scarcely mentioned (although pictured in Terry Moore's photographs). The politics of

development and commerce that so influence Baja and the oceans on either side of it are similarly given short shrift. Though I indeed care about the poor, the homeless, the refugees that inhabit the slums of the northern cities, as much as I do the traditional *vaqueros* of the sierras and the *pescadores* of the fishing villages, there is little urban political sociology in this book. In the end, I felt that the differences between the people of our own country and those living just south of the border were less than our similarities and that — in terms of our ties to ancestral landscapes and our declining communal natural resources — we were all in this together.

Of course, I had been a regular visitor to northwestern Mexico since the 1960s, beginning tentatively with Sonora and the Seri coast, then exploring the islands of the Sea of Cortez westward to the Baja Peninsula — a sort of reverse migration from the journey of the ancient Seri who probably paddled over from Bahía de los Angeles, island-hopping all the way to Tiburón.

In the spring of 1970 I was on the loose, still wandering two years after returning from the jungles of Southeast Asia, trying to get back into the countryside I had — before Vietnam — known as home. It was several years before I would take up filming and defending grizzly bears; I had time on my hands and was looking for an adventure. The father of my teammate Barry Spicer, fellow Green Beret medic in Vietnam, was a renowned anthropologist at the University of Arizona named Edward H. Spicer, a wonderful man who spent much of his field time among the Yaqui and Seri Indians of Sonora. I was still reeling from sixteen months in Vietnam and no doubt fit into one of those wacko categories later known as "walking wounded." At any rate, I mostly kept to myself and the wilderness; I had but few friends. One of these pals was Tom Hinton, whom I met through the Spicers, an ethnographer and professor of the people of north-western Mexico, who also taught at the university. One of Tom's students was a man my own age, Lloyd T. Findley, an ichthyologist who was curating the university's fish collection. Dr. Findley, who was still working on his Ph.D. in those days, had been a co-founder of the Sea of Cortez Institute of Biological Research; his thesis was in ecology and evolutionary biology, with emphasis in ichthyology, especially the family of fishes known as gobies. Professor Findley and I, along with Tom Hinton and Barry Spicer, all lovers of the Sonoran Desert, took many trips together, especially down to the Sea of Cortez on the Sonoran side. When Findley decided to go on a six-week collecting trip down the eastern coast of Baja California and visit many of the islands of the Gulf of California, it was only logical that I should accompany him. I signed on as driver, cook, mechanic, and bodyguard, and this slow voyage down Baja — before the roads were paved — with leisurely trips to gulf islands, became the bedrock journey to much of the peninsula that I had never before visited, and by whose perspective I came to gauge subsequent trips. Those desert places became magic touchstones I kept returning to. Even now I have a tendency to gravitate back to the same enchanted places.

Now, as I paw through this stack of notes and journals written around desert campfires, these names reappear: Dr. Edward H. Spicer, Dr. Thomas Hinton, Alexander Russell, and Edward Abbey — friends, mentors, great men of the desert — now all departed. Dr. Lloyd Findley, Omar Vidal, Yvon Chouinard, Peter Matthiessen, still with us. Any semblance of scholarship on my part is mostly coincidental and is totally the product of my association with these scholars, scientists, writers, and fine men. I have used many secondary references in compilation of human and natural histories of Baja and the Sea of Cortez. Those more interested in scholarly books should go directly to the source. I would suggest, for openers, consulting *The Sea of Cortez* by John Steinbeck and Ed Ricketts, and Joseph Wood Krutch's *The Forgotten Peninsula*. The latter title represents ten journeys of a civilized man; the former, a trip Ed Abbey might have taken had his life gone on another year. Ann Zwinger's *A Desert Country by the Sea* is a discerning work on the southern cape region. These are the popular classics.

Among natural history guides, *Reef Fishes of the Sea of Cortez*, by Donald Thompson, Lloyd Findley, and Alex Kerstitch, is one guide I always carry. A thinner volume, *Gulf of California Fishwatcher's Guide*, by Don Thomson and Nonie McKibbon, is the densest of all fish guidebooks. Richard C. Brusca's *Common Intertidal Invertebrates of the Gulf of California* is an uncommonly solid scientific work, although for practical clamming I am inclined to turn to *Shelling in the Sea of Cortez*, by Paul E. Violette. For plants try J. Coyle and N. Roberts's *A Field Guide to the Common and Interesting Plants of Baja California*, or

9

Frogs in the arroyo San Pablo.

Flora of Baja California, by Ira Wiggins. *Sea Shells of Tropical West America,* by Myra Keen, is another comprehensive work.

For the Sea of Cortez and gulf islands, there are two monumental works containing virtually all primary references available at the time of publication: the first is *Island Biogeography in the Sea of Cortez,* edited by Ted Case and Martin L. Cody; the other book, more specialized in that it deals with plant use on the Sonoran coast, is *People of the Desert and Sea: Ethnobotany of the Seri Indians,* by Mary Beck Moser and Richard Felger. *Tales from Tiburón,* edited by Neil B. Carmony and David E. Brown, now out of print, is a valuable reference.

A National Academy of Sciences memoir by Edward W. Nelson, *Lower California and Its Natural Resources,* is one of my favorites, not necessarily because of its scientific accuracy but because its descriptive passages were written from a perspective of more than a half century ago. Also, Homer Aschmann's *The Central Desert of Baja California: Demography and Ecology* is the definitive choice of knowledgeable friends.

The far-ranging collection of Dawson's Book Shop in Los Angeles, a small press specializing in Baja books, lists over thirty titles, many of them classics. Among them, *Cave Paintings of Baja California,* by Harry Crosby, is a good read for the odysseys of discovering great murals of the Central Sierra. Other references I have used are *Rock Art of Baja California,* by Campbell Grant; *Last of the Californians,* by Harry Crosby; and Randall Henderson's *Palm Canyons of Baja California.* I should also mention a novel, *The Journey of the Flame,* by Antonio de Fierro Blanco.

The written history of Baja begins with the padres. The titles I have used most frequently, and which cover most of the historic ground, are Clavigero's *History of (Lower) California,* Pablo Martínez's *Historia de Baja California,* Jacob Baegert's *Observations in Lower California* (1772), and *Baja California and Its Missions,* by T. Robertson. Arthur W. North's *Camp and Camino in Lower California* stands apart as a turn-of-the-century horseback exploration of Baja's extensive backcountry.

Maps are important, as are various travel guides, of which there are a number of good ones. The choice of maps is simple: the 239 maps of *The Baja Explorer Atlas,* available from 4180 La Jolla Village Drive, #520, La Jolla, CA 92037. Exactly which of the many guides is right for you depends on your own preferences, interests, biases, time and mode of travel; one must shop around some for the travel "voice" correct for you. The magazine *The Baja Explorer* (same address as above) carries a comprehensive list of books and guides for mail order.

Above all, I am indebted to my friends, those who have shared many adventures and campfires throughout the Baja region, among them Dan Sullivan, Mitch Wyss, Barry Spicer, Kim Cliffton, Terry and Suzi Moore, Rick Ridgeway, Dan Budnik, Fletcher and Claire Chouinard, and — my favorite campers of all — Lisa, Laurel, and Colin Peacock.

Finally, I would like to thank the Giants — the original inhabitants of Baja and the big islands of the Sea of Cortez. They are all gone now. But their descendants, the Paipáis and Kiliwas of northern Baja and the Seri Indians of Sonora, remember them. They say there were two kinds of Giants: the Giants of Baja, who were of enormous stature, and the Giants who lived on Tiburón Island and nearby. These Giants died off as a result of gambling debts — in which they bet their lives and lost. Others were changed into rocks and boojum trees.

The Indians of Baja told the Jesuit missionaries that these Giants were responsible for Baja's great cave murals, which depict eight-foot men painted on overhangs twenty feet off the ground. How else could they have gotten up there? It's the only explanation.

— Doug Peacock
Bahía de los Muertos
Baja California del Sur
Mexico
November 1990

in memoriam : Edward Abbey

introduction

by Peter Matthiessen

When I first visited Baja in 1946, by jeep, a poor road south from Tijuana went no farther than Ensenada, at that time a fishing village on the Pacific coast, perhaps sixty miles south of San Diego. I was nineteen then, just out of the navy, experimenting with beer and tequila, and all I recall of Ensenada is the blinding crash of the dawn Pacific at the end of a short street that ran down among the cliffs from the cantina. From Ensenada I traveled on cattle tracks to an old Indian village called Ojos Negros, in a broad valley beyond strange hills of huge smooth granites; from the far side of the valley a winding track — no more than a dark tracing in the stony earth — climbed through foothills of live oak and madrone and piñon to a high lonesome lake set about with white monumental boulders. The blue water was sprinkled with canvasback ducks, and except for the squall of piñon jays, the only sound was the sigh of wind in the ponderosa pine; a lone *vaquero* on a pony, raising his sombrero, was the one social occasion of that remote day.

Ruin and graves of San Fernando Mission, the southernmost Franciscan mission. The mission was founded in 1769 by Padre Junípero Serra.

Except for agricultural development on the Pacific slope south of Ensenada, most of the changes in Baja in the decades since have been confined to the far north and the far south — "the Cape," which is somewhat similar to the north in its oak-piñon-madrone highlands and relatively well-watered terrain. In between, the great mountain deserts that comprise most of a gaunt peninsula eight hundred miles in length — twice the length of Florida — remain mostly untouched even today. However, a paved highway from Ensenada penetrates the entire length of Baja, traversing the sierras through the old mission town of San Ignacio and continuing southward on the gulf coast beyond Mulegé, where it returns across the mountains to the Pacific slope before descending to the Cape. Until this highway was completed, in 1973, the great majority of the peninsula's population was confined to the northern border towns and those at the far southern tip, which were served by sea from Guaymas, Mazatlán, and San Diego. However, the new road is deteriorating, and full road service and spare parts — not to speak of respectable restaurants, motels, or inns — can be counted on only in a few places in the hundreds of miles between Ensenada and La Paz.

In 1984, I returned to Baja California by light plane, traveling south with my son Luke from Tucson, then Nogales, passing over the great mission at Caborca, then the empty coast at the north end of Tiburón Island and on across the long arm of the Pacific — known to the early Spaniards as the Vermilion Sea — that penetrates a thousand miles into the desert. The plane traversed the southern end of Angel de la Guarda Island and landed on the desert strip at the small settlement at Bahía de los Angeles, where we were met by Terry and Suzi Moore, Dan Budnik, and other friends. From there we made inland expeditions, and voyaged south through the Midriff Islands to our final destination, the great sea bird colony at San Pedro Mártir Island, a white spire of rock that is the most remote of all the islands in the gulf.

Now it is six years later, 1990, and we head south from Tucson on the old Nogales Highway, climbing toward the mountains of the border. To the west, under black hills, stands San Xavier, built by the Spanish padres about 1702 and still a Papago Indian mission. To the south and west is Madera Canyon, in the Santa Ritas, where the resplendent coppery-tailed trogon visits from Mexico. In early February, the Santa Ritas have a haze of snow, and the air is cold.

For this leg of our journey, "we" includes Doug and Lisa Peacock and their children Laurel, age eight, and Colin, who was barely unborn in 1984, the year that his parents and I first met in Tucson. That was also the first time I met Ed Abbey, in whose memory this book is put together, but mostly I talked with Peacock about grizzly bears.

Beyond Nogales, the road descends through rolling hills of piñon, pine, live oak and madrone into the flat deserts of Sonora — mesquite, paloverde, cactus, ironwood. To the west rise dark volcanic mountains of the gulf and, in late afternoon, the twin monuments called Goat Tits (Las Tetas de Cabra) that guard the deepwater harbor at San Carlos. The peaks are black against the setting sun, on the north rampart of the broad bay of Guaymas. From Guaymas, early next morning, we would take the ferry that crosses the gulf to Santa Rosalía in Baja California.

Blue-footed boobies,
San Pedro Mártir Island.

A bird island adjacent to
San Pedro Mártir Island,
Gulf of California.

School of dolphins at sunrise, Gulf of California.

Leaving the mainland coast, the ferry overtakes a vast school of dolphin that burst the white-capped blue seas in shining squadrons, driving sardines. The porpoise hundreds are attended by more hundreds of brown boobies, picking the fish bits that drift to the surface in their wake. Exciting as this tumult is, we have to wonder how much longer such spectacles would be seen, for the Colorado River that once fed the nutrient-rich waters of the gulf has been cut off by dams and canals in the United States and the Mexicali Valley, and meanwhile a Japanese-Korean fleet is hammering the gulf fisheries with long-line trawls and drift nets.

With Las Tetas high on the eastern sky, the ferry tends toward the west-northwest, to offset north wind and southerly current on this hundred-mile crossing. Off there in the northern mist, not so many miles away, lies San Pedro Mártir, the southernmost point of that earlier journey, and in all likelihood the nesting ground of the boobies and occasional tropic birds that cross our bow.

Toward dusk we come in under the peaks called Las Tres Virgenes, and stand off the Santa Rosalía harbor a few hours waiting for the tide. This ramshackle old town, which prospered a century ago in the days of the French copper mines, can claim a galvanized iron church designed by A. G. Eiffel of the famous tower.

That night, north of Mulegé, we drew off the main highway and made camp in the desert, sleeping on the soft white sand of an arroyo set about with palo blanco, paloverde, ironwood, and the elephant tree (Bursera), in addition to the great cardon cactus of Baja California.

On his earlier travels, someone had drawn Peacock a rough map of the old road to the great cave called San Borjitas, first described by the padres in 1772, and photographed in the 1890s by a Frenchman attached to the copper enterprise at Santa Rosalía. Next morning we followed a stone track inland, climbing toward the westward. Near the coast, the red floret of the bush ocotillo was the only note of color, and birds were scarce — a black-tailed gnatcatcher, an ash-throated flycatcher, a scrub jay, a shrike, all dry-billed insect-eaters of the low hot thorn and stone. But higher, in the canyon mouths of the Sierra Guadalupe foothills, where the cacti and shrubs and desert trees grew thicker and larger as they followed the arroyos into the sierra, there were black-chinned and black-throated sparrows, violet-green swallows, Gila and ladder-backed woodpeckers, and that great cuckoo called the roadrunner. Soon mesquite appeared, and small live oak, then figs, and with them doves and quail and flickers, and a mixed flock of brown towhees, cardinals, and the cardinal's close kin, the pyrrhuloxia.

A church built by Eiffel in the old French mining town of Santa Rosalía on the gulf coast.

At a small ranch twenty miles inland, in the mountains, in a dry woodland on the canyon floor, the rough track came to an end. From here we continued a few more miles on foot, in a still landscape of green bush, red cliff, and a ringing blue sky. Small caves began to appear in the narrowing walls and overhanging cliffs. At an old shelter with stone goat pens, under giant figs — silent but for the wing song, *whew, whew, whew,* of the white-winged dove — the canyon narrowed to a shadowed path among large boulders, only to open out again in a wild beautiful ampitheater ringed around with cliffs, and a strange great monolithic rock in its own pit at the very center — what Indian people would certainly treat respectfully as a "power place." Peering uphill through a phalanx of cardon cactus, I saw a figurative human, black and red, on the roof of a cave that opened out as we climbed closer, a vast hall some hundred feet across and eighty deep that might have given shelter to two hundred people. The entire cave roof, more than ten feet above the floor, was painted with large *mono* figures, most of them laterally divided head to toe, black on the left side, red on the right, and many pierced by one or more great arrows, with arms and fingers spread wide as if in pain. The figures all looked swollen, as in death. There were no hunting scenes, only a few random fish and deer and, on one wall, a series of vaginas.

On the cave floor lay numerous stone tools and turtle cores and also a half-dozen metates or stone mortars — used, Peacock guessed, for grinding out the dyes for the cave painting. Since San Borjitas has been known for more than two centuries, the undisturbed metates seemed astonishing. Fortunately this site is far out of the way. Even if one knows how to find the track, the hot slow jarring journey into the mountains, the long walk, place it beyond the ambitions of any except those who would respect it. Two beer cans and an empty box of army-issue cartridges — a hunter, we supposed — were the only evidence that modern men had been there, and the only sign of human presence we removed.

In 1984, we visited another remote canyon where beautiful wall paintings by an unknown "Old People" still survive. From an ancient lake bed, perhaps ten miles west of Bahía de los Angeles, a sand track left the improved road and headed southwest into the hills. One fork in the track was a dry wash of white sand leading south through beautiful dry country of immense cardon cactus, big-armed and bulbous, interspersed with the extraordinary cirio (*Idria columnaris*), known as "the boojum tree," which is found on Angel de la Guarda Island and at one location on the Sonoran mainland but is otherwise confined to a small range on this peninsula. Where red-purple cliffs convened to enclose this stream bed in Montevideo Canyon, the forty-foot cardons and taller boojums, set about with thick-trunked elephant trees, with

Cardon on the Llano de San Pedro. The cardon is the world's tallest cactus, sometimes reaching up to sixty-five feet in height.

18

Boojum tree (cirio) near Desengaño.

cholla and senita, crucillo and candelia, and stout barrel cactus up to ten feet high, formed a strange primeval forest in which a brontosaur would not seem out of place. An eighty-one foot *cirio* — the tallest known — grows in this canyon; it was a grown tree, in all likelihood, before the arrival of the Spanish padres. But here in Montevideo Canyon, so many of these peculiar growths approached that height that only a true connoisseur of boojums would distinguish it. The three orange tendrils of its candelabra or *cirio* were in strange spring blossom, as were many of the more ordinary desert plants — the yellow-flowered brittlebush and crimson feather duster, the blue and purple nightshades and verbena, a delicate mint smoked by the Hopi of Arizona (they call it *bunquitsi*), the orange globe mallow, white thistle poppy, and many other Sonoran desert forms. The desert animals were also familiar — black-tailed jackrabbits, a coyote, chipmunks and ground squirrels, an array of lizards, and a few red diamondbacks, one of which rattled so loudly that I heard the sizzle over the motor of our jouncing car. So were the quick lovely desert birds, the orioles and woodpeckers, verdins and gnatcatchers, attracted to the high cardons not only for perches but for nesting holes and sources of insect food and perhaps water. A Costa's humming-bird came to red blossoms of an ocotillo; a pileated warbler flitted through soft blossoms of the desert lavender; the black, shining phainopepla raised its crest in curiosity in the green branches of a paloverde.

The west side of the upper canyon was a red rock face with round-mouthed caves high up under the rim, well suited to aspirant shamans of Indian days. Some of the caves and higher crevices were marked by the white stains of hawk guano, revealing the location of past nests. Above the rim, in silver light, violet-green swallows crisscrossed the blue sky on the winds of March. On smooth rock walls where fires were once made in the canyon corners were priestly red figures with two horns and raised arms, surrounded by spirals and abstract designs in red, ocher, yellow, black, and white — much like the designs on Arizona canyon walls made by the Hopi, whose tradition speaks of an old homeland farther south. Since one design portrays a majestic corn plant, it seems unlikely that the vanished artists were the Cochimi people found here by the Spaniards, unless the Cochimi had retrogressed from a higher culture; according to the mission records, the treacherous Indians here were not corn planters but benighted hunter-gatherers.

19

Crimson fairy duster,
Las Arrastras de Arriola.

From San Borjitas we continue south, crossing the peninsula's one permanent river — the two-mile issue of a canyon spring of fossil water that flows down through dense palms like a long oasis to the gulf at Mulegé — and continuing onward to Loreto, where we make our camp off the old San Xavier Mission road south of the town. It was here at Loreto, in 1697, that Padre Juan María Salvatierre, crossing the gulf, founded the peninsula's first mission and settlement — the first, in fact, in all that vast western reach of the New World that was to become known as California. The Nuestra Señora de Loreto Mission — called "the Mother of Missions" — is the southernmost church on the old mission road, El Camino Real, that in the eighteenth century extended north to San Diego and San Francisco in Alta ("Upper") California, and also, on the Mexican mainland, as far north as the San Xavier Mission south of Tucson.

Río Mulegé
in late afternoon.
Date palms
flourish along the
peninsula's one
permanent river.

Nuestra Señora de Loreto, the first California mission, founded in the 1690s.

The gulf coast north and south of Loreto, with its high dark islands like brown ocean peaks rising gravely from the stone-blue sea, must count among the most striking in the world. In the eastern distance rises Santa Catalina, one of many islands in this "Sea of Cortez" with its own indigenous anomalies — in this case, a rattlesnake that lacks a rattle. Soon the road turns away inland, crossing the sierra and descending again to the Magdalena Plain on the Pacific slope. The west side of the plain is being irrigated with the last of the peninsula's fossil water, supporting the farm town of Ciudad Insurgentes (City of Revolutionaries) on Magdalena Bay.

Magdalena Bay is a vast lagoon more than two hundred miles south of Laguna Ojo de Liebre or Scammon's Lagoon, celebrated for decades among naturalists as a great breeding ground of the gray whale. At Scammon's, the cold water of the California Current turns west, away from the coast, which at Magdalena Bay is markedly warmer and less foggy. These days the whales are common here — so common, in fact, that half the town of Ciudad Insurgentes is out on the shore dune on this Sunday afternoon observing Leviathan sporting in the channel.

We hire a skiff that takes us some miles north to the tide rips of the channel mouth between the barrier islands, called Boca de Soledad, Sun Passage. Throughout this journey, whales rise and spout and porpoise on all sides, so close that we see the glisten of wet barnacles. Sometimes their great flukes, lifted clear before they sound, shed cascades of sparkling brine onto the surface.

North of the *boca* is a high dune island without track or path or any sort of habitation, and we choose our campsite in a dune hollow by the channel, more or less sheltered from the onshore wind. We set up tents against the heavy dew and, in the sunset, a few yards from camp, take cabrillas and a small halibut for our supper. At dark a brilliant orange moon comes burning up out of the east like a night sun and lays a path of gold across the water. In this far place, no lights are visible, no sound is heard — this coast appears entirely uninhabited. Behind camp, broad clear rolling dunes rise a hundred feet or more above the sea, and to the east, fringed by green mangroves, the desert extends to the smoky blue of the old volcanoes of the high sierra.

At Loreto we had picked up Yvon Chouinard, the celebrated mountaineer whose Patagonia outdoor clothing company is one of the few that has taken real corporate responsibility toward the environment. Tomorrow we will be joined by Dan Budnik and the Moores, together with children, friends, dog, and a rubber boat with outboard motor for our fishing.

In a red daybreak, in quest of driftwood on the ocean shore, I cross the high dunes of the island, which are a mile or more across, and bare of vegetation on the higher ridges. A fog drifts in from the Pacific, and the tracks of coyote seem mysterious, for there is no fresh water here, only the dew. On small knolls traced by tiny prints of mice and lizards and horned larks rise yellow primrose, lavender beach pea, a pink vetch. Here and there long-billed curlews send their sweet sad whistle through the mist.

With a length of rope, I bind up a cargo of firewood and hump it back across the island. The sea fog has crossed ahead of me and fills the channel, where two whales moving southward toward the *boca* rise with a soft puff and blow not thirty yards offshore, their spouts invisible in the sunny mist.

Prickly poppy flowers.

A beached whale on the Pacific side of a dune island north of Boca de Soledad.

In the afternoon, I walked south on the high dunes to Boca de Soledad. In the *boca*, just inside the outer bar, whales were so numerous that four or five mist spouts might be seen at once as the dark forms parted the shining waters of Sun Passage. Here and there, as if surfacing to ask how the world was going, a great cetacean head protruded, second after second, or a slow-raised fluke, or even a sudden upthrust where two-thirds of the whale's length surged clear of the swift tide before the huge weight crashed back in a white explosion in the channel.

Next day I walked back from the *boca* on the ocean shore, inspecting the myriad seashells from the Pacific. Happily, in this era of poisoned oceans, this outer beach is entirely free of inorganic litter — in fact, the only plastic that I saw was the upper half of a white bleach jug, a tool used commonly around the world to bail small boats. Flocks of shorebirds — plovers and sandpipers of several species — stood one-legged on the points in a hard wind, and in the distance a dead whale lay in the surf, attended by gulls and a pair of turkey vultures (a century ago, those vultures might have been condors). Swollen a pink-purple, the whale was still intact, its flipper jutting into the Pacific sky as rusty and barnacled as an old rudder. The coyotes would come to gnaw at it at night, and the crabs, copepods, and snails were already mining the vast trove of matter from beneath.

23

The weather is unsettled, no two days alike. Sun, rain, and wind. We cross over to the mainland shore and cast into the mangroves for grunt and snapper. Every supper we have fine fresh fish, for the fish here are still plentiful and unsophisticated, especially the cabrilla, a delicious rock bass, and even the children in the camp are expert fishermen.

My small tent sits between greened knolls on a dune of fine light pale sand above the channel. The sand is sprinkled with white shells of perished land snails, ten to the square foot, often many more, although there is no sign of live snails in the sparse dune cover. At the foot of the dune, along the water, a gifted crab or copepod creates an extraordinary spray of wet sand in its tidal excavations, its hole a mere pinpoint at the flower's base. From my tent each morning I can hear and watch the puff and blow of whales and dolphins; a young sea lion, as if anxious to be petted, haunts our shore.

On the last afternoon, in cool wind and shifting light, I walk north over the dunes, lost in so much solitude and silence. Small flocks of curlews whistle over the wheat-colored sand, as if preparing for the long flight north in a few weeks' time. Brant geese and white pelicans travel up and down the channel, sometimes a hundred brant in a single flock, or seventy or more of the rare pelicans. On the far shore, against the mangroves and the desert, stands a single egret, white as bone.

When the boat comes for us on the last morning, I ask the fisherman the name of our island. "No se," he says, looking confused. "No hay nombre." All this empty place, he tells us, waving his arms, is Magdalena.

From the coast we returned inland to the farm town of Ciudad Insurgentes, then south once more to Ciudad Constitución, both created in recent years at the expense of the receding fossil water. A few miles farther on, we turned off the paved road onto a rough track that led east into the foothills. (Because most of the interesting destinations are well off the main road, on tracks that dissolve without warning into old stream beds of soft sand or large rocks, strong four-wheel-drive vehicles — preferably two traveling together, rigged out with camping gear as well as racks for jerricans of fuel and water — are very useful for such travel.) On the north side of the road, the fenced-off desert was bright green; on the south side, the same landscape was dry-brown from too many years as open range for goats and cattle. Our destination was a palm spring oasis and the old church of San Luis Gonzaga, one of the last old missions on the Camino Real that are still standing.

In 1984, we visited San Borja, which stands perhaps thirty-three miles inland from Bahía de los Angeles, deep in the mountains. The mission of San Francisco de Borja was one of three bequeathed to the Church by Señora María Borja, Duchess of Gandía, who specified that they be constructed in the remotest parts of the peninsula. Accordingly, San Borja, as it is known, was founded in a remote mountain valley over twenty miles beyond the turn-off into Montevideo Canyon, beside a small spring that the Cochimi knew as Adac. Completed in 1762, the small adobe church roofed with palm thatch and tule served at least a thousand Indians who drifted in to live around the mission, and were doubtless conscripted to work in the mission gardens. For a time a shaman lit a bonfire before the church each evening in protest against the evil brought by the padres, and in fact the Cochimi resisted all religious instruction beyond what was required to insure them daily food, which, because of the meager water and poor soil, had to be supplemented by the other missions. The problem of hungry mouths was solved when the Indians perished of the diseases brought them by their benefactors. In 1773, the mission was turned over to the Dominicans, and in 1801 the adobe church was replaced by the larger church of stone that is still standing to this day. By 1818, when the Dominicans departed, less than one hundred Indians were left, and today the Cochimi, baptized or otherwise, have entirely vanished.

San Borja Mission, founded in 1759, is one of the best perserved and most remote missions in Baja. Only one family now lives permanently near the mission, which is southwest of Bahía de los Angeles.

Altar, San Borja Mission.

San Borja Mission.

After miles of rough thornbush and hot sand, the soft greens of the spring and the old building, faded pink, came into view around a slope of the brown mountainside; they cannot have changed much since the mission days. A caretaker's family in a small thatched hacienda farms the old garden between the adobe ruins and the warm, ill-smelling spring, which has attracted a variety of songbirds; the falling walls of the church compound defend his vegetables from the dogs, loose chickens, and archaic hogs. Formerly, the padres planted olives, date palms, pomegranates, grapes, and figs; these olive trees must be two centuries old. The peaceful building with its lovely old wood doors and cool interior, the still baptistery with its rays of sun-filled dust, the worn stone stairs to the small bell and the stone roof with its pleasant prospect of gardens and spring, the quiet farmyard and the silent mountains — there is a healing in such quiet, such isolation from the world. And yet there is a sadness to this place; one thinks of the doomed brown children in that baptistery, the shaman and his bonfire, casting his spells upon this house of God, and the lost voices.

We made camp perhaps three miles from San Borja, on a rise washed by cool airs from the Pacific. Next night we camped in an arroyo farther north. Near a spring that leads down to the ruins of the old Calamajué Mission, we flushed from the ground a large gray falcon, a peregrine or aplomado. (Flat cactus desert seems unlikely habitat for the rare peregrine, though we had seen it coursing the seabird islands off the coast; on the other hand, there are no records for the aplomado on the peninsula. Yet a friend of the Moores whom Terry regards as the most experienced field ornithologist working "the Baja" is convinced he saw an aplomado falcon only a few miles from this area, and my own instinct is that this bird was an aplomado. Nature study in this region is still incomplete, and for the student of natural history, there is still the possibility of fresh discovery, in a land that is almost untraveled more than a few hundred yards from the scarce roads.

27

Stairway, San Borja Mission.

Doorway, boarded up with boojum skeletons, San Borja Mission.

Like San Borja, San Luis Gonzaga, built in 1737, still holds masses on saints' days for the few near-Indians who dwell around it (some of them in the century-old green-gold mansion of the de la Tobas, who once, it is said, owned all this part of Baja California, from coast to coast). The old white church with its twin bell towers faces the great yellow Toba house and the palm springs, and its cool interior gives wonderful resonance to the murmured word. In the Spanish style, its spare white walls are littered with gaudy religious art, but otherwise it seems nicely suited to the stony landscape all around. In any case, San Luis Gonzaga is far more beautiful than the more modern "cathedral" at La Paz, the resort city in the cape region from where, two days later, I took an airplane up the gulf coast and across the Sonoran desert and the border to that former mission town of Alta California called Los Angeles.

From La Paz as far north as Loreto, there is no road along the gulf coast, only a few sandy tracks through the brown mountains known as Sierra de la Giganta to lone fishing shacks on the bare shore. As the sun rose, the mountains turned from brown to greenish gray. There was no lack of arroyos snaking down to the deep blue empty sea, but the rivers were sand rivers, pale and dead.

West of the sharp ridge along the coast, a highland of gray-green buttes and plateaus could be seen descending to the lagoons of the Pacific, a blue horizon in the early morning distance. The plane's crucifix shadow crosses small fields and the palm canyon at Mulegé, and peering, I can just make out the faint rock trail into the hills toward San Borjitas. From Santa Rosalía, the main road swings west toward San Ignacio, a pale scar in the mountain distance, and north of San Ignacio, on the Pacific coast, is the great San Ignacio Lagoon, then the famous Scammon's Lagoon on the farther side of the great Vizcaíno Desert.

Like the La Paz–Loreto coast, the gulf coast from Santa Rosalía to Bahía de los Angeles is stark and empty, long beautiful bays and shallow coves without harbors or any sign of man. Off to the east rises the white cone of San Pedro Mártir, then the Midriff Islands, and beyond, in full sun, great Tiburón Island and the Sonoran coast. Then Bahía de los Angeles appears, and with memory's eye I can make out the lightly tarred and lightly traveled road that wanders out of town past such makeshift enterprises as an auto repair shop that also served as butcher shop and bakery, past the weedy air strip road, past the mongrel pack that disputes with ravens at the roadside dump. The road curves uphill and heads inland, forty miles or more across the cactus, sage, and greasewood reaches of the high Vizcaíno Desert to the north-south highway.

The San Luis Gonzaga Mission was built by Johann Jakob Baegert in 1752. He described the Indians as "always in good spirits, they laugh and joke continuously; they are always contented, always joyful, which without doubt makes for real happiness — what all the world strives for and few achieve."

The town of San Luis Gonzaga with the mission and its related buildings on the left, and, on the right, a grand house built by Don Benigno de la Toba in the mid-1800s.

The plane flies the length of Angel de la Guarda Island, a few miles offshore. Already, as the morning grows, the peninsula is turning the pale dusty brown of ancient desert stone. El Picacho del Diablo, highest mountain in Baja at 10,154 feet, commands the range called San Pedro Mártir. The blue of the great gulf is turning pale, as the plane nears the vast delta of the Colorado, which no longer nourishes the gulf; already the fish populations and bird colonies have begun to die. All that is left is this broad salt mud wandered by vague tidal rivers. To the west, among those mountains, lies the beautiful blue lake with the white boulders, first visited more than forty years ago.

In 1984, on the way north, I retraced that journey and was sorry. Ensenada today is a small hot tumultuous city, a good paved road leads east to Ojos Negros, and what once must have been a sacred lake of the Indian peoples is now the heart of a new Parque Nacional named for Mexico's 1857 constitution. The track out of Ojos Negros was almost as rough as it had been forty years before, but a litter of human activities crops up at the park border, and recent visitors — no doubt kin to those who hang beer cans on ocotillo plants and toss old tires over the columnar cacti — have invaded the blue lake to paint their names in bright loud letters on its old white rocks.

Overleaf: Dawn, Bahía de los Angeles.

¡baja!

prologue

During February of 1977 I found myself alone on a desert island lying ten miles off the coast of Baja California. Famed desert bush pilot Ike Russell had dropped me off, landing his souped-up Cessna 185 on a makeshift swath of runway hacked through the brittlebush that covered the *bajada* (the desert playa) just above the sea cliffs. Ike was the only person known to have attempted a landing on the island, once clipping off his landing gear on a guano-covered offshore rock, crash landing later at Caborca, Sonora, alive but battered. Ike had flown here five days ago at the request of my old friend Edward Abbey, who had chartered the pilot's services to cover a magazine assignment, which was to be written by Ed and photographed by Terry Moore. Ike had flown Ed and the others back to Sonora the day before, leaving me alone. Ike remarked that he had to return to fly a lizard biologist over to Bahía San Luis Gonzaga on the Baja mainland ten days from then, and, if I was interested, he could pick me up on the way back. For me, it was a dream come true: camping alone in the desert by the sea — the essence of everything I loved best about Baja and the gulf islands, this marriage of ocean and cactus. The gas and Ike's expenses — along with my ten days of solitude — were Ed's gift to me.

And if there was ever a time I needed such a gift, this was it. Nothing acute, just the run-of-the-mill midthirties metaphysical doldrums, when the whines of indecision ruled — who to be, where to go, what to do, whether to go on — all the sniveling of a subadult male who has yet to commit to anything or hold down his first job.

The first day I made camp at the foot of the sloping alluvial fan where the plane had landed, not wanting to haul the forty-pound jerrican containing my five gallons of water any farther down the beach. My biggest problem would be finding drinking water on this arid island, which was said to be entirely without fresh water. But in fact I knew of a palm canyon twelve miles to the south where Ed Abbey had discovered a large natural tank of water that would last until summer, when the heat would dry it up. Since — given the rugged terrain and treacherous scree of the island — it would take me at least three days to hike down and haul water back to my pickup spot, I planned on conserving my water supply, making it last for ten days.

35

A black chuckwalla sunning on a cardon, Mejía Island.

San Pedro Mártir Island, Gulf of California.

Food was another small problem. I didn't bring much and had consumed most of my measly larder by the time the others flew away in the Cessna. I had some coffee, a bit of powdered milk, and a small bottle of Mexi-pep. This situation was not troubling, however, as the land and sea offered a varied commissary, and gathering it would be a challenge. The agave cactus were prime for harvest and there were large, black chuckwalla lizards of the *Sauromalus* genus, tremendously ugly, but no doubt quite nutritious. Beyond the desert lay the Gulf of California, where even the most inept of fishermen could eke out a living.

I rolled out my sleeping bag on a gravelly bench twenty feet above the coarse winter beach and began looking around for wood for a fire, Not much grew on the *bajada* besides the brittlebush and an occasional creosote bush. Elephant trees occupied the slopes of the nearby hills but I knew from experience that their wood — like that of paloverde trees — burned poorly. I gathered some thin twigs of creosote, then scrambled down the rocky terrace to the beach and collected a small armload of driftwood.

The tiny fire threw a few faint sparks into the gathering darkness. I stared into the embers of driftwood, which emitted small eruptions of green and red flames — the result of traces of metals absorbed from the ocean. The long winter night closed over the land and Orion rose beyond the clamor of barking sea lions coming from a narrow granitic island somewhere to the northeast. I took a deep breath and savored the approaching days of austerity and solitude — my annual shot at simplifying my life and giving my tired and abused body a rare dose of good health.

On the morning of my second day, I began exploring around, looking for the perfect spot to set up a base camp. I was only a couple of miles from the northern end of the big island and everything I had with me was crammed into my big Kelty backpack. What I wanted was a place on the beach above a white crescent of sand with a great view of osprey-nested headlands, offshore islands, a spot with abundant shellfish at low tides, and a supply of firewood sufficient to steam open all the clams and mussels I cared to eat. In short, an idyllic campsite — not unreasonable expectations given any number of wild coastlines along the gulf coast of Baja.

37

Wildflowers.

Elephant tree and cardon, Cerralvo Island.

Osprey nesting in cardon, San Lorenzo Island.

A long finger of volcanic rock ran off into the pale, flat ocean — indistinguishable from the morning sky. Beyond, a white islet where cormorants roosted seemed to float on the horizon, an illusion drifting randomly on an empty canvas of sea and sky. At the end of the little ridge on a bump of hill was an osprey nest. I scrambled up the ridge, then turned away from the sea and climbed higher for a view of the surrounding country. Not a hint of breeze moved the paper-thin filaments of bark hanging to the trunks of elephant trees. I thought I heard a distant gasp coming from far out on the ocean. Grabbing my binoculars, I glassed the horizon until I caught the black of a fin — a bottle-nosed dolphin, I thought — then a spray beyond and another fin too large for a dolphin. In the next few minutes I watched the white spouts of what seemed to be about four different fin whales blow into the fading gray of the morning sky. A bit to the south was the darkness of another land mass, probably Tiburón Island near the Seri coast. In the opposite direction, a mile up the coast, a shelf of black rock covered with sea lettuce was emerging from the falling tide. Just

38

beyond the flat of black and bright green was a quarter moon of sand — the camp I was seeking.

I filled my water bottles from the five-gallon jug, shouldered my backpack, and picked my way through the rocks, arriving at the small beach by late morning. The tide had just started to come back in and about a hundred feet of intertidal sand was exposed. I dumped my pack and pulled off my boots and trousers, hanging my sweat-soaked clothing on clumps of saltbush. The short though rigorous hike had me breathing hard; the life I had come here to transcend was slowing me down. I pinched the roll of fat around my middle: I would do something about that before returning to Tucson.

A number of circular, five-inch-wide white shells littered the upper reaches of beach. The seashells were lovely, a thin lacquered exterior with crowded, flattened, concentric ridges — a big Pismo-like clam. Smaller members of the same species lay open and picked clean on the lower beach; some kind of animal was eating the handsome bivalves. I waded out into the surf, the salt water cool and soothing on my bruised feet. A small explosion of water startled me, and a foot-wide ray skated away. Not wanting to impale my foot on the barb of a sting ray, I retreated to the sands just above the incoming tide. I squatted and dug a hole in the sand with my hands. There were lots of little holes in the wet sand, and I figured some of these had to be the siphons of clams.

39

Angel de la Guarda Island, Gulf of California.

After fifteen minutes of digging, my hands were raw and I had not found a thing. I gave up on my clam dinner, but didn't lose sight of the fact that I was hungry, without food, and my best shot at easy pickings was going to be shellfish at low tide. I wasn't ready to try for a chuckwalla yet.

I retreated to my pack and got out a beat-up pair of tennis shoes to protect my tender toes, then walked up the beach to the next outcrop of rock, working my way along the basalt just above sea level. I wanted to check the tide pools out for something to eat.

A red rock crab scurried out of sight at the tip of the headland. The wind had picked up slightly and waves were rolling over the tide pools, hindering visibility. Attached to the rocks were anemones, small limpets, and a few blue mussels. I twisted the mussels until they loosened, then pulled the beards from the rocks. The biggest of these mollusks was only about two inches long. I kept at it until I had a baseball-capful.

That evening I set up a little camp in the lee between two miniature sand dunes. Standing up, I could look out over the beach to the shore a hundred feet beyond. There was no shade, but that would be no problem until the next morning. Behind me the tangle of halophytes provided lots of small kindling for the fire, and larger pieces of driftwood could be picked up on the beach. There were probably lots of rattlesnakes in the thickets when the weather warmed up.

I propped a quart-size aluminum pot between big cobbles and added an inch of seawater. When it boiled, I dropped in the mussels and covered the pot for three or four minutes until they steamed open revealing the orange interior of the cooked invertebrate. I added a few drops of Mexi-pep and pulled the wound-colored mass from the pearly inside of the shell. I thought it a delicious meal.

Daybreak. Dew coated the leaves of saltbush and had soaked through the foot of my sleeping bag. I kindled a small fire, then warmed my fingers on my frijole-can coffee cup filled with the precious black liquid and watched the sun rise out of the Sea of Cortez. The morning was cool (the temperature was probably in the low sixties), so I grabbed my binoculars and a quart of water, stuffed a snake-bite kit in my pocket, and struck out for the west coast of the island, no more than a mile distant. I aimed for a low pass and picked my way through the sparse scrub vegetation. A few elephant trees, paloverde, torote, and treelike ocotillo decorated the lower slopes. Up higher and steeper were organ-pipe cactus and groves of larger cardon cactus of an unusual growth pattern, the likes of which I had seen nowhere else. But in fact, everything living on each of these gulf islands is a bit unique, having evolved on these volcanic peaks sinking in the ocean and isolated for millions of years. On another island, three hundred miles to the south, are rattleless rattlesnakes and ten-foot-high barrel cactus — species not found elsewhere. Farther south, on a smaller island, melanism has prevailed in a singular species of black jackrabbit living among gray andesites and scabrous vegetation.

Rattleless rattlesnake on Santa Catalina Island.

41

"More clouds emerge from empty sky, anvil-headed giants with glints of lightning in their depths. An armada assembles and advances, floating on a plane of air that makes it appear, from below, as a fleet of ships must look to the fish in the sea."

Edward Abbey

Sunrise, Bahía de los Angeles.

At the little pass I stopped and looked out at the Ballenas Channel. A couple of miles out in the strait lay a pointed rock that looked like a sail. A swarm of seabirds — gulls, terns, blue-footed boobies, and pelicans — dove on baitfish just beyond the little island, which seemed to be suspended in midair; only the roosting seabirds anchored the mirage to the surface of the ocean. Closer in, an osprey circled a headland. To the north was an islet connected to the mainland by a neck that you could cross over at low tide; I avoided the headland because brown pelicans nested there and I didn't want to disturb the active rookery. At my foot were a number of white, elongated animal droppings, which puzzled me until I realized they were the scat of the big black chuckwalla lizards. There were no game trails because there was no game; the only land mammals, besides bats, seemed to be mice and some larger species of rodent. Along the rugged coastline rose rotten cliffs of decomposing volcanic rock which fell off steeply into the sea. I had hoped to find a point of land or a big rock from which to fish with a hand line, but no such possibility was to be found there.

I spent the remainder of the day looking for food. At low tide I waded out, shuffling my feet along the bottom to avoid stepping on a sting ray, but again finding none of the large handsome clams. The tides here were complex, and I was just beginning to get a handle on them. There appeared to be four daily tides, two lows and two highs, which I watched closely, pegging the highs and

lows with creosote sticks. The two highs and two lows were unequal; one was always higher or lower than the other. The tidal range from the lowest low to the highest high might have been ten feet. I think the proper name for this pattern is "semidiurnal irregular." This information was important to my daily routine, because most of my food gathering was intertidal, and much of my travel was conducted below cliffs at low tide. When the tides were high, I would have to scramble up into the treacherous scree and rotten volcanic rock, climbing up and down the fluted terrain, an endless landscape of gullies. Not only was travel time increased by a factor of four, but I ran the risk of breaking a leg or running into a rattlesnake with no one on the horizon to call for help.

I gathered another hatful of mussels, finding some big ones just under the low-tide level on the rocks closest to the sandy beach. I walked back into the desert checking out the cactus, but the only fruiting ones were barrel and a much smaller cactus of the pincushion variety. The fruit of the barrel was, I knew, next to inedible. The elongated fruit of the smaller cactus was tiny and waxy, red instead of yellow, but tasty within the bland tradition of desert winter gathering.

In order to conserve my water supply, I used seawater for everything except making coffee; I cooked with it, washed with it, and even drank mouthfuls whenever I craved salt — every half hour or so when trekking down the beach at midday — diminishing my fresh water requirement down to about two quarts a day.

43

Cardon cactus, detail.

La Vela, a popular roost off the northwest side of Angel de la Guarda.

Each night I would savor a precious cup of warm water, flavored with a thin tablespoon of powdered milk, as I frugally burned driftwood and watched the constellations emerge in the winter sky. Venus would appear, and shortly thereafter I'd find Orion, then the Dog Star, and maybe Ursus Major and Polaris. Later, on the opposite side of the North Star from the Big Dipper, the great square of Pegasus stood clear in the darkening sunset of the western skies. I had brought along a page cut from a *Natural History* magazine, which showed all the constellations of the northern hemisphere in winter. It was one of those star charts you had to look at upside down and turn according to the month of year and the hour of evening. Once I got used to it and plotted Orion and Polaris, always easy to find, it was simple enough. I had long been familiar with the flashier signs of the zodiac — Taurus, Gemini, Leo, Virgo, Scorpio, even the harder-to-discern Cancer and Libra and my own sorry-ass birth sign, Aries, a tiny shapeless blotch of insignificant stars — but now I began discovering constellations whose names were unknown to me. I'd wake several times during the long hours of winter, roll over in my dew-covered sleeping bag, and check the incoming stars, rolling in on the celestial clock, against my chart, using my little flashlight. Each night I'd add a couple new constellations to my growing list.

The fourth day was a landmark during my island sabbatical. The bigger low tide of the diurnal cycle was the first one, coming just before noon, as I would guess by my compass. The tides had been getting bigger each day as the moon waned down to a thin crescent coming up just before sunrise. I knew the biggest tides rolled in during a full or new moon and that the next few days would be my best days for digging clams. I was determined to locate the habitat of the big Venus clams. Each morning I planned my day around the pattern of tides. What I most looked forward to was my daily forage on the tidal flats, when I would strip off my clothes and walk in the gentle surf, traversing the small beach many times, now armed with a sharpened pole that had floated in on the waves, following the receding flow out into the bay, shuffling my feet, and poking the stick into suspicious depressions in the sand, wary of sting rays.

Many small holes of various shapes dotted the beach; most were smaller than a dime and on the sands exposed during lowest tides. I figured that these were mostly the holes of worms or siphons of clams. I inched along in the little waves of slack tide, dragging my bare feet along, knowing from experience that the sting rays didn't injure you if you kicked them from the side. I examined each hole, as I had on the previous days, wondering which ones represented which kind of critter. Every now and then I'd see a tiny spout from a siphon hole and would pounce on it to dig for the clam or cockle I never managed to find. Overhead, a line of pelicans flew toward a roost. The osprey, who had been my fishing companion most of that morning, departed for her nest. Looking down, four feet away, I saw a pair of siphon holes close together with something white in them. The holes were almost touching, little tangential circles. I stepped toward them, and the white disappeared. Stooping and kneeling over the spot, I dug with my fingers in the sand. Five inches down, I felt something hard. My fingers closed over a large clam shell. I pulled it out, then washed it off in the sea. It was a beautiful white clam almost six inches in diameter — a big dosinia of the Venus family of pelecypods. I held the clam in my right hand and turned into the sun, my arms outstretched, my head thrown back, naked as a *Sauromalus*, grateful in the winter sunlight.

After that pivotal moment, I found dosinia clams with ease, effectively solving my food problem. The double siphon hole was distinctive. Actually, close up, it was more like a crenellated hourglass. The crucial thing was that the white stuff meant a clam's siphon was right at the surface, and these big suckers were slow diggers. If you saw the siphon, you invariably got the clam a few inches under the holes. Treading softly was important, since stomping your foot caused the clams to retract and disappear.

44

A row of pelicans gliding over water at sunrise off Angel de la Guarda.

Within an hour of finding the first, I had enough clams to last for a couple days. I carried them back up the beach near the high-tide mark and buried them in a three-foot-deep hole I dug with my sting ray spear. I figured that since the big bivalves were such slow movers, I could use the ocean beach as my live-box, a kind of marine refrigerator, redigging them at my convenience on the upper beach.

In about four days of wilderness solitude, something happens to me. It doesn't matter if I'm in the Cabeza Prieta desert, a wild ridge in grizzly country, an expanse of Arctic tundra, or here on a lonely beach of the coast of Baja. My senses gradually tune into the land around me, transporting my point of view outward, paying less attention to myself and more to the natural rhythms around me. Sometimes I try to imagine the lives of birds and cactus; it doesn't always work but it tends to render self-indulgence impossible — an effective Zen therapy for whimperers.

46

Reddish egret landing in mangrove.

The next morning I rose at daylight and ran on the beach, which was totally out of character. I have never been a jogger of any sort, and though I value a functional strong, healthy body, running for recreation or for the sake of exercise has always bored the hell out of me. I save the running for times when things big, bad, or armed are after me. But that morning, no such aversion applied. I ran naked at the line of surf caressing the shingle from one cliff to the other — about a quarter of a mile — then turned around and recrossed the crescent of sand. I ran and ran for nearly an hour, pausing only to swim in the chilly sea to catch my breath. The experience was incredibly energizing, a sensate physical joy first burned into my brain in childhood, when, a six-year-old boy, I would play Indian in the north woods of the Great Lakes, shedding my clothes to run wildly through the brilliant maples and sumacs of October.

From then on, I ran every day on the beach, about an hour in the morning, and again for another half hour in the afternoon. I couldn't get enough of it. Never before or since have I done such running. My belly fat melted away almost perceptibly now that I was a hundred miles removed from the nearest beer store.

Actually, I found cans full of beer on the deserted beaches of the island. Each day I explored as far down the island as I could get, skirting below the sea cliffs at low tide. The cans had washed in from who knows where — probably fishing boats, shipwrecked *vagabundos del mar,* or *bandito*-ravaged Gringo pleasure boats. I scoured the beaches, finding a total of five beers on four different days; two Tecates, two Budweisers and a Coors. All shared the same defect: a tiny hole around the pop top had allowed the carbonation to escape, and this leakage provided the buoyancy that floated them in to my beach. The beer was flat and warm, but beer — the only show in town.

I pulled on my clothes and hiking boots. I wanted to hike down the island before the tide rose and covered the beaches at the foot of cliffs. My activities were dictated by periods of the tides, cycles of a single great wave, pulled and pushed by the moon and sun, whose empirical patterns anyone living attentively on the beach could discern in a few days. I shouldered the Kelty pack containing water and emergency items, and climbed up the rocky ridge. My feet were now so toughened by running that I needed the boots only for rock climbing. I had only two more days on the island before Ike Russell would return, and I wanted to try to climb the highest peak. Ike had told me he saw boojum trees up there at about

four thousand feet from his plane. These cousins of the ocotillo are one of the most distinctive plants on the continent and their distribution is limited. The boojum (*cirio*) is found only in the central desert of Baja, from below El Rosario south to Guerrero Negro on the Pacific and the slopes of Las Tres Virgenes on the gulf, and again, across the gulf, on a narrow strip of coast just below Libertad, Sonora, where they grow on the wetter, usually northeastern, slopes of the mountains. Of course, if you were to draw a straight line from one area to the other — and this is exactly the direction the dominant winds blow wayward birds — you would intersect this island.

I left the coastline before midday and climbed for two hours up the side of the highest of the two peaks on the north end of the island. The scree was horrible: rotten, decomposing volcanic tuffs.

47

A field of lupine.

I glassed the slopes and could make out what looked like stunted boojum trees on a ridge. Turning back, I headed down into a little valley, passing one rose-colored rattlesnake, several of the big chuckwallas, and a field of waist-high lupine in flower. I reached the sea cliffs, but the tide was still up, too high for travel. I had seen a green sea turtle in this lovely bay on my second day alone. Digging into the backpack, I drew out a snorkel — fashioned from flotsamed hose — and mask, shed my clothes, and kicked off from a big rock into the bay to pass the time. I paddled out along the rocky spine. A host of brightly colored blue and orange fish glided over the rocks. There were a dozen or more species of little ones. I saw a cornetfish, triggerfish and a small school of sierras. At the tip of the rock I dove at some stripes in the rock and came nose-to-nose with a big zebra moray eel who scared the hell out of me. I turned into the bay, seeing one ten-pound black grouper and several cabrillas a quarter that size. The tide was dropping, so I headed in. On the sandy bottom in a fathom of water were sting rays, big eagle rays with five-foot wing spans, lots of them.

Slack tide was still two hours off, so I baited a hand line with a mussel and weighted it with a stone. The line was wound around a beer can and I whirled the stone around my head a couple times and flung it out, pointing the Budweiser can out and letting the monofilament strip off the makeshift reel.

On the fourth cast I got a nibble. I struck the fish and was fast to a two-pound cabrilla. I hauled the fish in, with little interest in sport; I wanted a break from the monotony of my shellfish diet. I quickly filleted the small bass, packed away my gear, and headed back up the beach to camp.

Two days later, when the inevitable intruder sailed into my cove, interrupting my island solitude, I wasn't bothered in the least. Though far from lonely, I was receptive, feeling that his arrival was as ineluctable as the tides. The intruder was a high school biology teacher from California and he knew both Dr. Findley and Dr. Brusca. A small world, I thought. We fished from his dinghy until noon, when Ike Russell's Cessna touched down on the *bajada*.

Osprey in flight.

49

California sea lion with pup, Granito Island.

Sunrise over San Marcos Island.

creation of the baja peninsula and the gulf of california

The Baja Peninsula is one of the most striking physiographic features on earth, especially when viewed from space. Longer peninsulas exist, such as the Malay or Kamchatka, but none extends down eight hundred miles but averages only some seventy miles across. This elongation, accentuated by the blues of the pounding Pacific and the relatively tranquil Gulf of California — also known as the Sea of Cortez and the Vermilion Sea — catches the eye because there are seldom clouds concealing its mountainous spine and lovely coastline. Baja and the Sea of Cortez are inseparable phenomena: neither exists without the other. They are the Siamese twins of plate tectonics. Their climate, physiography and island biogeography are interdependent.

Just before being drafted for Vietnam I completed an undergraduate degree in geology at the University of Michigan. Back then, geology was less a science than a right-brained exercise in intuition. The students really good at math and science went into engineering. The crackpot notions of continental drift and sea-floor spreading were presented as part of a one-hour lecture on the theoretical history of geology. The grade school concept of fitting Atlantic South America into western Africa was a child's notion not worthy of further discussion.

But times and minds change, and today that harebrained idea, plate tectonics, is the fundamental theory explaining why the face of the earth looks the way it

does. The slow shearing of the nine or so very large, sixty-mile-thick plates composing the earth's crust explains the origin and present shape of the oceans, the growth and ages of mid-oceanic ridges, of coastal and continental mountain ranges, most volcanic activity, submarine trenches, and sea-floor spreading such as the bottom of the Gulf of California.

Baja and the Gulf of California originated four or more million years ago when the peninsula began separating from the mainland of Mexico. Most of the islands in the Gulf of California are transported geological remnants of this clash of tectonic plates, with lower California drifting off to the northwest. Baja, the Sea of Cortez, and its islands are all the result of this continuing process.

51

Salt formations in Estero de San José, near Guerrero Negro, Pacific coast.

Sal Si Puedes Island, one of the Midriff Islands.

The actual age of the gulf, its islands, and the Baja Peninsula are subject to some interpretation. The age of the basalt on the ocean floor at the mouth of the gulf indicates that the major part of the peninsula started to pull apart four and a half million years ago. But millions of years before, the ocean invaded this basin area of what used to be part of the basin and range province. Until perhaps twelve million years ago, streams draining the northern Sierra Madre ran southwest to the Pacific. Then, the area now containing the gulf subsided, interior basins were created by erosion, and an arm of the sea invaded. Islands may have been isolated by inundation several million years before the Pacific and North American plates began to separate at the northern extremity of the East Pacific Rise along a complex of faults, including the San Andreas, during Pliocene and Pleistocene times. The geothermal heat flow of the East Pacific Rise continues today on the ocean floor.

The cape area south of La Paz could have been a Pliocene island. Later, during Pleistocene times, the Gulf of California was much longer than its current northwest-trending axis of 669 miles. Shortly after its Pliocene origin, the northern gulf covered the Coachella and Imperial valleys and extended north of present-day Palm Springs; the delta of the Colorado was somewhere around present-day Yuma, Arizona. But

sedimentation in the Colorado River delta dammed off the Imperial Valley, and the river flowed alternately to the open sea or westward into a saline basin. Later, the river dumped into the dry lake basin, creating Lake Cahuilla, which probably drained into the gulf by way of the Río Hardy.

The land of Baja and the Gulf of California is largely desert; most of the peninsula's fifty-four thousand square miles receives less than ten inches of rainfall a year. In the lands bordering the gulf, only the Sierra Kontaak on Tiburón Island catches enough subtropical moisture to support thorn scrub vegetation; the remaining areas lie in the Lower Sonoran Life Zone, a desert land making the Gulf of California the only evaporite basin of the Pacific Rim. The mountains of northern Baja, especially the pine-covered, ten-thousand-foot San Pedro Mártir, gather in more rain and snow, as does the Pacific coast in the form of ocean fog. As one drifts south, toward the cape, occasional hurricanes rake across the peninsula, and violent Caribbean squalls, known as *chubascos*, belt the entire gulf region. On the ground the rainfall can vary immensely with parts of the lower desert and some gulf islands going years between measurable rainfall.

53

An aerial view of San Lorenzo Island,
Gulf of California.

"Through the long desert day the sunbeams are weaving the skeins of color across the sands, along the sides of the canyons, and about the tops of the

mountains. They stain the ledges of copper with turquoise, they burn the buttes to a terra-cotta red, they paint the sands with rose and violet. . . ."

John C. Van Dyke

Sunrise along the Sierra San Pedro Mártir, with Picacho del Diablo, at 10,154 feet the peninsula's highest peak.

The physiography is basin and range with subdivisions. In the Gulf of California, those physiographic divisions include the Colorado River delta, the Midriff Islands, and the central and southern portions of the gulf characterized by long transform faults and deep basins and some impressive submarine canyons. The spine of the Baja Peninsula is mountainous, the higher ranges lying to the north. The Sierra de Juárez and San Pedro Mártir are granitic, with steep easterly escarpments that, adjacent to the 10,154-foot-high Picacho del Diablo, fall off to sea level in a few rugged miles of rapidly descending, palm-studded canyon. Farther south are a broken series of ranges and dissected plateaus: the Sierra San Borja, Sierra San Francisco, Sierra Guadalupe, and Sierra de la Giganta — the ranges of the Central Sierra. South of La Paz, in the cape region, rise the subtropical forests covering the Sierra de la Laguna.

Below the tablelands are lowlands. East of the northern ranges lies a low area spotted with ancient playas. The Magdalena Plain and Vizcaíno Desert region around Laguna San Ignacio constitute the other two great lowlands.

Along the west coast of the Baja Peninsula are a number of large bays or lagoons; San Quintín Bay is the northernmost of the large ones. Midway down is Scammon's Lagoon, then, around and south of the prominent nose of Punta Falsa, is Bahía San Ignacio, and finally, down the southern flank of the peninsula, the complex of bays and channels around Bahía Santa Magdalena. There are other bays and lagoons, but these are the big ones, and are well known as gray whale–watching areas. They are also important geographical references, whether one is navigating a sailboat or merely glancing at a map. For example, the temperature of the ocean changes north and south of Scammon's Lagoon, with temperate species of marine animals found to the north and tropical ones to the south. This boundary is, of course, gradational. Bahía Tortola, a small bay just south of Punta Eugenia, is where — on a journey south — one first finds tropical inshore invertebrates outnumbering temperate ones, in number of species if not biomass. By the time you reach Bahía San Ignacio, there are mangrove forests, and once you pass Bahía Santa Magdalena, the temperate species disappear nearly altogether. More visibly, as you go north, around Scammon's Lagoon, where the colder California Current sweeps nearer the coastline, you find forests of giant kelp, abalones, elephant and harbor seals, and assemblages of kelp fishes.

On the gulf side of Baja, typically tropical species are found farther north, although temperatures can be complicated by strong currents, regional and local upwellings, impressive tides, and local geographical features. One notices the lack of giant kelp beds, goose barnacles, and extensive mussel beds, though some goose barnacles and

Looking west at the Sierra de la Giganta, southwest of Loreto.

mussels are found. A number of temperate species are, in a manner of speaking, trapped in the upper gulf where waters are cooler. The *vaquita* is perhaps the most spectacularly "trapped" or "disjunct" animal because of this mammal's rarity, the fact that its geographic range is the smallest of the cetaceans, and the notion that it may be a Pleistocene descendant of a coastal porpoise that once ranged from the Gulf of California down the Pacific coast of South America. But there are others; fish such as the totoaba, sharks, corvina, and other "twin" species also found off the Pacific coast.

Cholluda Island, Gulf of California.

Overleaf: The Midriff Islands — San Lorenzo Island at sunrise with San Esteban Island in the midground, and Tiburón in the distance.

The peninsula from Cerralvo Island, the gulf's southernmost island.

The gulf between San Esteban and San Lorenzo Islands at sunset.

This sketchy evolutionary history of the Baja Peninsula includes the arrival of *Homo sapiens,* and ends, in my mind, just before the arrival of the Spanish, whose introduction of European diseases marked the end of traditional people in Baja. This does not mean the Western man stands apart from the selective processes that have brought us to this critical juncture. Only, that in this particular desert peninsula, the mechanisms of change before and after the arrival of the first white men were quite different: the natural selection of Darwinian evolution was gradually replaced by human-induced processes to such a degree that, toward the end of the twentieth century, one could argue that vertebrate evolution had — for all practical purposes — come to a halt, and that the only animals much larger than small birds and reptiles who would continue to share the planet with us would be those of our own selecting.

The first people to reach the region now known as the Baja Peninsula were relatives of the first people on the Californian coast, and all these people were probably descendants of four North American women who stood on the Alaska side of the Bering Strait some twenty-three to eight thousand years ago. Both the Bering land bridge and a travel corridor south through the interior of western Canada were probably open from 17,000 to 18,000 B.C. and, again, after 12,000 B.C., a date that better fits the uncontested cluster of radiocarbon dates associated with Clovis Man. Although

Seri Indian, Berta Estrella Romero, holding an iron-wood eagle with Tiburón Island in the background. The Seris still fish and travel across the gulf from Sonora, occasionally reaching Baja California.

62

much truck has been given to Polynesian islanders floating over to Peru on balsawood rafts and latter-day arrivals by Nordic Vikings, it now appears that some 95 percent of American Indians are genetically linked to this tiny band of early Arctic explorers. Studies of mitochondrial genes, which are separate from other genes and passed on only by mothers, allow scientists to track the diversity of these energy-producing genes backward over hundreds of maternal generations to these four hardy women. Only the more recent arriving Athabascans, Eskimos, Aleuts, and postcontact immigrants trace their heritage elsewhere.

Exactly when these people wandered down this arid and rugged peninsula from the rich and comparably gentle country of mainland California is unknown. Much of Baja is yet terra incognita in terms of its known prehistory. Two fluted Clovis-type spear points reported from the Central Desert of Baja California suggest that the peninsula may have been occupied as early as eight thousand or even ten thousand years before Christ, the time of the San Dieguito or, slightly earlier, Llano complex (these are tool assemblages). What happened in between the time of these few bands of big game hunters and the European contact in 1532 is anybody's guess. At the time of contact the indigenous population was estimated at sixty thousand. The material culture seems to be at all times largely Paleolithic or nonagricultural; the combination of exploitation of marine resources combined with desert-culture hunting and gathering provided a subsistence economy.

Despite our ignorance concerning Baja's prehistoric inhabitants and our inability to penetrate the inner lives of these vanished peoples, the leavings of their material culture are all over the place. Everywhere you go, there is stuff on the ground — flakes, projectile points, shells, metates, grinders, scrapers, choppers, and a complement of bone tools. Beyond these utensils of everyday life lies the magnificent rock art, the great painted murals of the central mountains. What richness these ancient leavings lend to the landscape — a sense of pleasure and depth of time. Man has known the enchantment of Baja's coastlines and sierra for thousands of years. The traveler to the peninsula who picks up a flaked stone tool should feel the kinship inherent in the artifact, then return it to the sands. It is better left where it lies. These relics of lost cultures are perhaps more valuable

as sources of inspiration and reminders — that we were not the first, nor will we be the last, to pass this way — than as the sum total of all conventional tidbits of scientific information.

The classic cultural progression of prehistoric American Indian from highly mobile big game hunting (Paleo Indian), to local hunting and food gathering (archaic), and on to agriculture seems not to apply here. Baja's original inhabitants appear to have gotten stuck somewhere in the middle. At a time when empires were being built in Mexico, Mesoamerica, and South America, and civilizations established in the Pacific Northwest, Baja California remained in the Stone Age. It seems to have always been a cultural backwater. And, in many ways, it remains so today.

63

An elephant tree growing through a lava flow below the volcanos, Las Tres Virgenes, northwest of Santa Rosalía.

notes from a desert playa (a brief history of baja)

"The weird solitude,
the great silence,
the grim desolation,
are the very things
with which every
desert wanderer
eventually
falls in love."

John C. Van Dyke

One winter, fifty miles north of my campfire here on the eastern foot of Sierra San Pedro Mártir, somewhere around February of 1828, mountain man James O. Pattie and his band of trappers nearly perished in the sands of Laguna Salada, southwest of present-day Mexicali. He and seven others had worked their way down the Colorado River by canoe and horseback, trapping beaver in the rich bosque and brackish waterways. At the delta, the muddy river waters braided into myriad channels lined by thickets of willow, cottonwood, and mesquite. Great fleets of snow geese, sandhill cranes, and cormorants soared above rafts of mallards, avocets, willets, and widgeons, while herons, egrets, hawks, and owls hunted the banks. There, the trappers' horses were stolen by Indians. They buried their heavy loads of pelts and started walking west across Baja. The blaze of sun on the alkali dust of Laguna Salada blistered their feet. Not a single shrub decorated the salt flat, and they soon realized they must reach shade by morning after their third night out and find something to drink shortly thereafter or run the risk of death. The men knew this was possible because they could see snow on the higher elevations of distant granitic mountains, and the irony of dying of thirst in view of snowbanks drove them on.

After three days without water they reached a canyon in the Sierra de Juárez, a mountain range rising to the zone of pines on the northern edge of the Baja Peninsula. A broad canyon of boulders and stunted palm trees narrowed to granite walls where clear running water cut a narrow white swath through the heart of the bedrock. On the coarse damp sands along the creek were the prints of deer, sheep, cougar, and smaller wild cats for which they knew no name. Two days later, in a thicket of oak and agave stalks, they sighted a silver-coated bear, an *Oso plateado* or *Oso grande*, just across the divide.

That wild landscape visited by Pattie and his men — the first Americans to see this land — complete with its exotic megafauna, faded from human memory before anyone recorded its passing: the lush jungles of the lower Colorado teeming with waterfowl and game, visited by the California condor, by Mexican wolves and jaguars. On the west side of the Sierra de Juárez, above the mission of Santa Catarina, roamed grizzlies and mountain lions who lived off mule deer and mountain sheep. Pattie's report of the grizzly bear is the only record of a bear on the Baja Peninsula. That does not mean bears were rare or absent: the chaparral and montane habitats of the Sierra San Pedro Mártir are the ecological equivalent of areas in the southern and central parts of the state of California where a more complete written history demonstrated that such regions teemed with grizzlies.

65

Sunrise on Laguna Salada with the Sierra de Juárez to the east.
The Laguna Salada almost reaches the U.S. border west of Mexicali.

"The colors, like everything else on the desert, are intense in their power, fierce in their glare. They vibrate, they scintillate, they penetrate and tinge everything with their hue."

John C. Van Dyke

66

Sunrise on Laguna Salada
with the Sierra Pinta to the south.

The Baja that Pattie and his men knew seems unimaginable and unknowable, a landscape generating dreams far from those of this seemingly tame hunk of desert playa on which I have unrolled my sleeping bag. Yet it is the same place, much of it unchanged in two centuries, the essence of Baja: the desert rising out of the sea. The peninsula he saw was the most richly diversified bioregion on the continent; nowhere else were there so many different kinds of animals in such a small region. The combination of montane, chaparral, riparian, thornscrub, desert, littoral, and marine habitats provided an ecological range of plants and animals seen no place else in North America.

I poke at the embers of a mesquite fire with a creosote stick, waiting for the moon to rise. The moon is two days past full, and I am camped on a fossil sand dune less than fifty miles south of where Pattie saw the grizzly bear. Except for the passing of those big carnivores, the charismatic megafauna, the land looks much the same as it did in 1825. Except for a few tiny *rancherias,* no one is out here; as far as the eye can see, there are no lights or visible sign of humans. These dunes are on the western edge of another playa lake several rocky passes south of Laguna Salada and at the foot of the escarpment of the San Pedro Mártir, which reaches straight up to the zone of fir trees and beyond into a November sky rapidly filling with stars in the fading light. The vertical relief here must be close to ten thousand feet; the scattered clamshells of the *Chione* genus suggest the dunes are close to sea level, though I am some thirty miles inland from the Gulf of California. Alongside the shells are fire-broken rocks from the hearths of ancient fires and grinding surfaces rubbed into the convex sides of large granitic cobbles. Not much grows here besides the clumps of creosote and mesquite amid the hummocks of dune. The larger trees appear to be a *Lysiloma* of some kind.

I have come out here alone to the desert of northern Baja to try to distill a feeling for the land and its history, to listen again to the pulse of its animals and plants — an elusive quest. The modern story of Baja California, of this desert place by the sea, has always seemed out of sync with the biological richness of the land; outsiders have always considered this coastal desert country unspeakably harsh, unproductive without the importation of water, food, and energy. Western man has always been the fish out of water here, apart from this land so strange and hostile. The last tangible remains of those not estranged from the land may be these fire-broken rocks and granite metates. If this were Australia, Africa, or another desert area where traditional cultures persisted, I might have sought the answer to some of these quandaries among the tribes and clans of native people. But, with the exception of some Cucapás on the Colorado and a few families of Paipáis, Kiliwas, and Tipais hidden away in the northern sierras, the original inhabitants of Baja — the Indians — were wiped out by diseases brought from Spain four hundred years ago.

69

Rainbow at sunrise, Sierra Pinta.

Pitahaya ágria with flower.

I have not heard a sound since dusk, when the drone of a single engine aircraft drifted in from the east, toward San Felipe. Now, just as the moon rises out of the dry lake bed, the cries of coyotes shatter the silence. Though Pattie's slice of Baja — complete with the richness of the big predators — is no more, at least he was at home with the country as I am here in this great desert valley. Others were not so comfortable with Baja's rugged terrain, strange and sparse vegetation, and unforgiving heat. A repeated theme one hears is that the indomitable toughness of Baja has rejected or shaken off the civilizing efforts to exploit the land by conquistador, missionary, whaler, geologist, and developer. Maybe so.

The first Europeans landed in Baja in 1533. The ship, the *Concepción*, was built by Cortés and launched under Captain Diego Becerra, who was murdered by his own crew. His pilot, Fortun Jiménez, sailed the ship into La Paz Bay and set off inland for water. While they were on land, Jiménez and twenty-two of his crew were killed by Indians. The surviving Spaniards reported seeing beautiful pearls; thus Cortés was back with five hundred soldiers in the spring of 1535. Disease, tropical storms, and the unending hostility of the Pericue and Guaicura Indians drove them out less than two years later.

Cortés tried once more to find a beachhead in Baja. He sent Francisco de Ulloa, a noted navigator, up the gulf to the Colorado and around Cabo San Lucas as far north as Cedros Island in 1537. Unfortunately, Ulloa was murdered by one of his companions; his charts and notes were lost for a century.

Others, such as Juan Cabrillo, continued the exploration of the Baja Peninsula. In 1596, one of the most competent of the early explorers, Admiral Sebastián Vizcaíno, set sail for Cabo San Lucas, then up the coast to La Paz, where the Indians gave them pearls and pitahaya fruit — a prophylaxis against scurvy. They continued rounding the cape northward to central California, where they saw dozens of grizzly bears feeding on a whale carcass in Monterrey Bay. Vizcaíno got as far north as Mendocino in present-day California. The maps drawn by him and his cartographer, Martínez Palacios, were the best available for two hundred years. Unfortunately, Vizcaíno mysteriously fell out of favor with the governors and was exiled to Sinaloa, and Palacios was beheaded for forgery.

The colonization of Baja began in 1697, when Jesuit Padre Juan María Salvatierre, filling in for Eusebio Francisco Kino, founded the mother mission at Loreto. These sixteenth-century Spanish missionaries were the first to record their impressions about the land: "Everything concerning California is of such little importance that it is hardly worth the trouble to take a pen and write about it. Of poor shrubs, useless thorn bushes and bare rocks, of piles of sand without water or wood," wrote the Jesuit Father Baegert. Father Venegas found it "a land the most unfortunate, ungrateful and miserable in the world." Later, Father Link wrote: "nothing but rocks, cliffs, declivitous mountains, and meaningless sandy wastes, broken only by impossible granite walls."

Still, no one could question the dedication of these devout men whose stark monuments still grace the peninsula as lovely ruins. Despite their failure in the conversion business (although they managed to baptize a number of the some thirty thousand aboriginal souls who succumbed to European-introduced disease before death sent them to the hereafter), the padres' strengths and feats were often legend. At the mission of San Xavier, Father Ugarte's great physical strength kept order; he wrestled unruly Pericue parishioners and once he took out a mountain lion armed with only a stone. Later, in 1751, when German Father Baegert couldn't find a ship, he simply rounded up a crew of Yaqui warriors and sailed over to Loreto in a dug-out cottonwood log.

San Xavier Mission in the Sierra Giganta, southwest of Loreto, is one of the grandest missions in Baja.

Bell, San Xavier.

San Xavier Mission.

Cristo at Nuestra Señora de Loreto.

Santa Rosario at San Xavier.

Two boys in a doorway, San Xavier.

Much later, beginning in the 1850s, other Europeans explored the west coast of Baja, scouring the region for whales, elephant seals, and sea otter until, by about 1890, these marine animals had been hunted to the point of extinction. For these Yankee seafarers — such as Captain Scammon and his crew — the central west coast of Baja must have seemed as strange a landscape for whaling as any they had seen on their many voyages from the Arctic to the South Seas; the gray whales who came here to mate and calve used the shallow waters of lagoons shoaled off from the Pacific and surrounded by ghostly white, shifting sand dunes. Still, the whales were here, and in abundance. Scammon was only the first to discover the lagoon now bearing his name. Others joined in the hunt until, some thirty years later, few gray whales were left.

At the same time, the colonization and settling of Baja continued following the collapse of the mission system. Mexican independence from Spain came in 1821. General merchantmen sailed up and down the coasts. Soldiers from the missions melted into the growing population of immigrants. In 1843, the governor declared that the mission lands should be given to the Indians, but by this time the natives were all but extinct. The California gold rush of 1849 drained off a good part of Baja's population and few of these returned from Alta California.

The remaining people farmed, ran livestock, fished, or mined. Near the middle of the nineteenth century, the American adventurer and filibusterer William Walker invaded the peninsula; fellow countrymen J. Ross Brown and, later, Arthur Walbridge North prowled up and down Baja looking for enterprising ventures.

In the Central Sierra, along the backbone of the peninsula, frontier ranch families settled in. The ranch life of the interior is perhaps the most viable and enduring of cultural traditions in Baja. These people became known as the Californians, and it is here that the traditional fabric of ranch life survives much as it was lived during the past two hundred years. The carrying capacity of the central sierra, based on the traditional agrarian life, is such that the area could not support a larger population. Hence, these families became severely inbred and, by the second half of the twentieth century, recessive genes were showing up: deaf mutes, a tendency toward hypertension, babies with extra digits and mental deficiencies.

Agave plant, detail.

Adobe ruins of Santa María Mission, founded in 1767, the northernmost Jesuit mission. No one any longer lives near the mission.

Mural at El Palomar, Santo Tomás Valley.

Las Coronelas, a classic Tijuana bar.

A ladrillo brickmaker in Mexicali Valley.

A burro cart photographer in Tijuana.

Virgen de Guadalupe, a roadside shrine east of Ensenada.

Sara Espinoza, a Kumiai Indian basketmaker,
at San José de la Zorra, in the northern mountains.

Paipái Indian potter, Manuela Aguiar, at Rancho Escondido.

Paipái Indian graveyard, Santa Catarina.

A playa south of Laguna San Ignacio.

"The very air here is miraculous, and outlines of reality change the moment.
The sky sucks up the land and disgorges it.
A dream hangs over the whole region, a brooding kind of hallucination."

John Steinbeck

I toss the last big piece of mesquite on the fire, thinking that the isolation of the Californians has ended, as it has today for most other inhabitants of this once-forgotten peninsula. The moon is climbing high in the eastern sky and it is so bright out here on the sand dunes that I can almost, but not quite, write by moonlight. I have pulled a folding chair from my pickup and sit comfortably in front of the fire. A tin cup in the sand beside me holds a nightcap of tequila. It is quite civilized out here in this remote valley. Actually, within a hundred miles of here, a million people live in Mexicali and Ensenada. Tijuana has over a million more, many of them recent arrivals, including political refugees from Central America. Ensenada, anchored in good farmland and commercial fishing, has grown more modestly than Tijuana in the direction of tourism. Giant salt-evaporation fields surround Guerrero Negro and smaller ones operate on the islands of Carmen and San José in the gulf. Around the Magdalena Plain, industrial irrigated agriculture is sucking up fossil groundwater; salt water is already migrating inland, reclaiming the bulldozed desert fields. Paved roads now carry tourists and sport fishermen along both coasts and all the way to the cape, where a festoon of concrete headlands and garish resorts suffocate what were the loveliest beaches on the continent.

Not all modern commerce has damaged the natural habitats. Today, it should be noted that, having been all but exterminated, the primary species of large marine mammal Scammon hunted, the gray whale, has made an impressive recovery and is now believed to be at or close to historic numbers. Mexico has in fact enacted conservation measures designed to protect a number of marine species including the gray whale, elephant seal, Guadalupe fur seal, sea turtle, and totoaba.

This does not mean all is well in the present-day marine habitats of the Sea of Cortez or in the Pacific region of the Baja Peninsula. Gigantic factory ships flying Japanese, Korean, and Taiwanese flags and using drift nets, seine nets, and long-line fishing technology are having a serious impact on longbill, squid, and other pelagic fishes. In the Gulf of California, especially the upper gulf, the indications of overharvesting the resources are even more ominous. In the spring of 1990, one of the principal researchers of the gulf reported that the fishermen themselves — who work out of the villages of the northern gulf — know, even as they daily speed its demise by overfishing with gill nets, that their way of life will be over in a decade, because in ten years there won't be anything left to fish for. Again, the ancient story of men killing what they best love, hastening the end of the only life they know, just as Pattie's men brought about the end of the mountain man era by trapping off the beaver and bringing in the settlers who plowed under forever the way of the free trapper.

The fire has burned down to orange casts of mesquite, the moon is overhead, and I have been into the tequila a bit too heavily to be talking about human dialogue with the land without feeling a tad pompous. Still, this persistent and disturbing tendency of *Homo sapiens* to overharvest their backyards is troubling, and some other night I will have to work on the problem of whether man can live in the world without destroying the natural systems that put him there.

"To survive is natural," I blurt into the night, raising my cup to the moon and draining the last of the Herradura. The desert sky is enormous, truncated in the west by the dark shadow of the Sierra San Pedro Mártir, the silence across the playa immense. For me, the earth is once more complete and I imagine the value — greater than any need to fuel or feed the world — of these wild desert lands and coasts lies their solace to nurture that most basic of human instincts. I unzip my sleeping bag and slip in for the night. I pull my stocking cap down over my eyes, blocking out the pale brilliance of the nearly full moon. Then I am asleep.

Laguna Diablo, December 1989

81

A roadside "sculpture" and roadmarker south of
Laguna San Ignacio, near the Pacific coast.

the central sierra

Despite all the talk about the harshness of Baja — the land rejecting the yoke of human development — man's relationship with this desert land has not always been antagonistic nor is it everywhere estranged. Perhaps the best examples lived — and still live — in the Central Sierra. Before the Spaniards arrived, the Indians of Baja, such as those of the interior sierras, lived within the parameters of the natural environment; without, as far as we know, altering or damaging the physical environment. Theirs was essentially a stable and static desert culture for some six thousand years.

The merit of this stability or value of this way of life depends upon the viewpoint of the observer. The Spanish missionaries were not charmed.

The German Father Johann Jakob Baegert, who lived at Gonzaga Mission in the 1750s and '60s, wrote:

. . . of people who, besides their physical shape and ability to think, have nothing to distinguish them from animals. . . . Gratitude towards benefactors, respect for superiors, reverence towards parents, friends or relatives, politeness with fellow man, are unknown to them, and words for these attributes are not in their dictionary. Laziness, lying and stealing are their three hereditary vices, their three original sins. They never work, never bother about anything except when it is absolutely necessary to still the pangs of hunger.

Or as Miguel Venegas wrote in 1759:

The characteristics of the Californians, as well as of all the other Indians, are stupidity and insensitivity; want of knowledge and reflection; inconstancy, impetuosity, and blindness of appetite; an excessive sloth and abhorrence of all labors and fatigue; an incessant love of pleasure and amusement of every kind, however trifling and brutal; pusillanimity of every thing which constitutes the real man, and renders him rational, inventive, tractable, and useful to himself and society.

A couple decades later, the Italian Father Clavigero wrote in his *History of (Lower) California*: "They are uncultured, very limited in their knowledge through lack of ideas, lazy through lack of stimuli, inconstant, hasty in their resolutions, and very inclined to gambling and to childish diversions through lack of restraint."

Many, including the missionaries who left written accounts, conclude the indigenous people's lack of "progress" reflects some failure of effort or imagination. But Baja California is also a tough and demanding land, where — given a level of technology such as that of hunting and gathering — the physical environment itself imposes limitations on material culture or even social and ideological matters.

These observations of Jesuits and other early Europeans are representative of the low opinion they formed about the native inhabitants of the peninsula. These poor Indians of Baja got a bad rap from the padres, even worse than the missionaries' accounts of their other Indian wards in the

Manuela Arias Pico Romero, whose family has been caretaker of Santa Gertrudis Mission for years, holding a statue of the saint. The clergy abandoned the mission in the early 1800s.

Santa Gertrudis Mission.

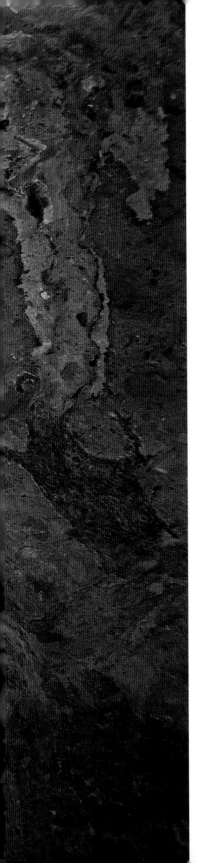

colonial Christendom of the Southwest or the northern California coast.

Yet one could as easily imagine these Baja Indian men and women happy, blessed with the fullness of days, gathering the richness of the desert, living in the most benign of North American climates, listening to the mountains with the practiced attentiveness of the hunter, receiving the gifts and wisdom of the land.

What belies the Jesuit theory of low spiritual nobility among the prehistoric savages most compactly can be seen in the rugged mountains of the Central Sierra. Here are found mysterious rock paintings of larger-than-life-size desert bighorn sheep, deer, whales, lions, and men in hematitic ocher, splashed by ancient Indians on overhangs of dacite and other rock. Nothing quite like this is found anywhere else on the continent; it is a unique North American art form. These Indians painted the rock with the timeless and universal concerns of fertility and abundance — the essence of survival. Here in the sierra, this cosmology was mixed with daily considerations of extremes of heat and scarcity of water. That they transcended whatever life — and one could imagine it a rich one — they lived in this land of extremes and diversity, and that they independently created a great art tradition, speaks to all of us of new possibilities.

Anthropologists are not quite sure what to think of these paintings; for example, these large figures are often painted over with other animals, possibly, they think, expressing power or domination over the animals. The disappearance or scarcity of game may have triggered the paintings. Yet overpainting appears to encompass every succession of figures, human or animal.

Another possibility is that, in the vast majority of murals, overpainting has had little or no relationship to the previous painting. Whatever was represented or undertaken was for its own sake, not for what came before, and certainly not for posterity. No one had lasting art on his or her mind when he or she went into the caves of the Central Sierra to slap these giant dreams on the rock.

Pictographs at Cueva Pintada along the arroyo San Pablo, Sierra San Francisco.

Pictographs at Cueva Pintada along the arroyo San Pablo, Sierra San Francisco.

On the Baja Peninsula, these questions about native people living in harmony with the natural world go unanswered. Indians fell victim to Spanish diseases and firearms before anything was recorded about their way of life. The people of today's Baja are the descendants of immigrants.

Although my first trips into the Sierra San Francisco were taken for the usual reason — to see the great murals of a forgotten people, I soon realized that I had yet to scratch the surface of my real curiosity about the place — the lure of the land itself. I wanted to walk across that flat-topped mountain range, drift across its high mesas, then drop down into its rugged canyons, well watered and studded with palm trees, and follow them out onto the blistering *bajada* twenty-five miles away.

This is a trip I have yet to take, although the land is there, largely unchanged in two hundred years, and a traveler needs only the time to do the walking. The Sierra San Francisco gets more visitors these days now that the government has declared the region an Archaeological Zone. Not only does this legislation give the local people a vested interest in protecting the paintings, but the Californians — should they choose — are wonderfully suited to the task. A repeated theme of the past century of exploration and history of Baja: these mountain people, the Californians, are the friendliest and most hospitable on the

Pictographs at Cueva Las Flechas, Sierra San Francisco.

88

peninsula or in the entire country. Gustav Eisen, writing in the 1890s, said: "As regards the people, it can be said that they are very friendly and hospitable; there is not the least danger to anyone and even the most inexperienced traveller need have no fear." And Harry Crosby, who journeyed these lands looking for the great murals, in 1981: "There has been little cruelty and less crime. Among these people there is a real concern for reputation, an esteem based more on a person's character than on his material success."

Today, the local people act as guides to the painted caves, and are compensated according to a fixed rate, specified in the regulations that govern this National Park land. It seems dignified work. Most of the best known murals are located in the canyons draining the Sierra San Francisco. Access is by either of two dirt roads from the south. One ends near a tiny village named Santa Marta, the other, at San Francisco. Most visitors take the graded San Francisco road, that breaks off Highway 1 twenty-eight miles northwest of San Ignacio.

Despite increased tourist visitation to the Central Sierra, there remains a surpassing sense of timelessness with each visit. On my most recent trip to the Sierra San Francisco, Dan Sullivan and I took the rugged Santa Marta road. We

arranged at the village for a guide, Patricio, who was of the Arce family that settled the area almost two hundred years ago. He noted that there wasn't a lot of work up here in these mountains and even hiking the *barrancas* with strangers beat walking the thirty-some miles for a *ranchero* Saturday night in San Ignacio. We agreed to met Patricio at the village of Santa Marta the next morning.

We camped in the upper palo blanco–lined sands of the Arroyo de Santa Marta. Darkness closed over the land suddenly without the slow parade of colors seen from beaches and playas. Deep in this broad canyon of the interior sierra, the stars shine more brilliantly than anywhere else on the peninsula. A coyote barked and, as we turned in, two great horned owls called from down the arroyo.

Patricio waited outside the little museum and we drove in the pickup a mile or so north to a *rancheria*. From there a goat trail climbed up to a low pass. Palo blanco and paloverde trees blanketed the canyon bottom and white-winged doves startled, bursting from the thickets of wolfberry every minute or so. Black-tailed gnatcatchers buzzed the sloping terraces of elephant trees, *Lysiloma candida,* and *Pitahaya dulce.*

The cave was at the base of a cliff and the easiest way to reach it was to start at the pass and contour back west. We passed a small painted cave with some deer and big fish and eleven tiny deer, outlined in white and painted in black, running in a synchronous line as if each

89

were a single frame of a strip of animated film. Next came Palmarito itself; life-size deer, a black mountain lion, and more than a dozen of the outstretched human figures, many with headdresses, a couple with gigantic biceps. Two giant red deer stood face-to-face; others were pierced by spears or arrows. There were the usual leaving of obsidian flakes and a few monos perhaps for grinding paint pigments.

From this overhang known as Palmarito, you could look out southward over the dissected tableland of the Sierra San Francisco. Though the great canyons presented problems to navigation, I thought how easy and pleasant it would be to walk the summits and ridges of this great mesa. On the skyline loomed the dark peaks of the Cerro Encantando and Sierra de Guadalupe. I once visited those mountains fifty miles south of here during the summertime; this is a different country altogether during the summer heat. The summer weather of central Baja is hot, exceedingly hot and humid; only the monsoon softens the hammer of sun on the volcanic anvil of the Sierra de Guadalupe. These sudden torrential rains scour the canyons and cleanse the washes, insects hatch and birds feed, and, as if by miracle, the earth turns green. The summer thunderstorms mark the renewal of life; the land is reborn and the desert year begins.

Roncho Pozo Aleman, an old mining area near El Arco.

The purpose of my summer visit was to see one of the great cave murals; the scene on the roof of that cave, like the neighboring cave at San Borjitas, was one of death. San Borjitas shares with Palmarito the distinction of having been both centers of prehistoric art and, later, of mission activity. Hence, both sites have been known in the historic record since the 1770s. San Borjitas lies near the mouth of a small canyon only about thirty miles northwest of Mulegé, past a deserted *rancheria* with goat pens fenced in to giant fig trees. The canyon then narrows and the trail — only a goat path — climbs steeply up the south side of the *barranca*. Below the pitahaya and palo blanco–covered slopes is an inner gorge, a thicket jungle penetrated by an occasional fan palm.

The cave doesn't look like much. If the trail were not there, you might bushwhack right on past without noticing it. The cave is upslope, at the foot of a cliff of dacite, and eighty feet deep. Some eighty figures, life-size and bigger, mostly human but also fish and deer, are painted in red, black, white, or half red and half black across the ceiling of the cave. Fifty of these stiff, slightly bulbous human figures are painted frontally with outthrust

arms — like fat gingerbread men. The biggest men are eight feet long, some with headdresses, arranged in random orientations, as if floating like autumn leaves caught in an eddy. All have their arms outstretched and many are impaled by arrows, some carefully painted to show feathers and arrowheads. Only women and a crosshatched scarecrow figure — apparently the oldest of the paintings — have been spared this symbolic fate.

A few white fish up to six feet long are painted over figures at the back of the cave, and a single life-size deer. But the great art on the ceiling of this cave is not about hunting. It is an unmistakable death scene. The figures are bloated, as in death from the desert heat, penetrated by as many as six spears or arrows. The mural might be about sorcery or war: the homicidal panorama seems to be of a pitched battle, though Indians were not known to wage such warfare.

At Palmarito and the other cave sites in the Sierra San Francisco, the paintings feature life-size animals — mostly deer, sheep, and fish — and suggest themes of hunting and magic. Not far from Santa Marta is a place known as "Cueva Sinuosa," the only recorded instance of a plumed serpent in Baja. Some scholars think this might suggest influence from the

mainland of Mexico — sort of a reverse migration of ideas from the probable trip of the original Seri Indians. At any rate, the zone of these large life-like paintings seems sharply delineated. The great representational cave art of Palmarito is found as far south as Mulegé and as far north as San Borja. (At Arroyo Montevideo, west of Bahía de los Angeles, there are two smaller figures of the representative type.) North and south of there, the prehistoric art tends to be more abstract.

A single image lingers from the central sierra of Baja. Years back I visited one of these caves during the monsoon. I was alone and a great blizzard of butterflies filled the canyon bottom — a snowstorm of variegated insects as high as the cave and only a bit less wide than the valley itself. Then a thunderstorm rolled through and I watched a flash flood rage down the arroyo. Shafts of sunlight pierced the clouds and steam rose from the cliffs and ledges. Fragments of clouds hung below the rim. It began to warm up. As I turned to leave, the butterflies started to come back out, swarms of yellow and white wings disappearing into the scudding clouds and reemerging on the other side as a gasp of color.

Converging canyons in the Sierra San Francisco.

Cabo San Lucas, Land's End.

traveling

If there were one rule about traveling in Baja — and there is none — it would have to do with time. The more time you have, the more flexible you remain, the longer you linger, the slower you go, the better. Walking is best. To really see the country, sense its morphology, to feel its breezes, savor its heat, and smell the fetor of the land, it is best to be on foot. Others prefer to ride horseback or to take mules and burros into the sierras. On the water you might travel by kayak, or even paddle a canoe along the beaches and around the headlands, carefully watching the patterns of winds, weather, and tides. Again, the more time you take off your travel time to a preselected destination in order to dive, snorkel, fish, or beachcomb, the better. In a land so big and rich and diverse, what you get depends on your curiosity and the duration of your attentiveness.

Of course, it is a true luxury these days for modern travelers to be handed this leisurely an agenda. We usually blast on down the highway in our various rigs. On other occasions, we can only take off enough time for a round trip ticket to Loreto or La Paz or Cabo San Lucas to charter a weekend *panga* and try to hook a yellowtail or dorado or sailfish with a fly rod. If you are a pilot with a tough little plane and are not afraid to attempt near-blind landings on remote dirt runways, you can drop in on countless small strips all over the peninsula. Again, you need time and a few phrases of Spanish to extend your explorations beyond the airfield. Those of us coming down on an ocean charter will be moving slow enough but with little individual free time really to see the place. You get dumped at a mission or market or maybe cruise into some *boca* to see a gray whale.

A mildly romantic sense of adventure is not inappropriate here. Most classic twentieth-century journeys down the peninsula were undertaken with a sense of anticipation, exploration, and even mild foreboding. Joseph Wood Krutch opens his fine book, *The Forgotten Peninsula,* with his dilapidated truck stuck in the sands of El Mármol. Erle Stanley Gardner pioneered the use of helicopters thirty years ago, skimming along the rims of the central sierra looking for Indian cave painting — long before these flying locusts became toys to the rich and irritants to the earthbound. The classic trip by sea was made by E. F. (Doc) Ricketts and John Steinbeck in 1940 aboard the *Western Flier;* one might manage to duplicate this journey, but you would be hard pressed to better it.

93

For most people, traveling down Baja means driving a vehicle. This is not a bad way to see the country. You need not to place too many constraints upon yourself, because the more interesting places are always a bit off your route. That "route" is normally the 1058-mile two-lane pavement of Highway 1, "Numero Uno," the Transpeninsular Highway of Baja. Along the highway, and in some of the villages and towns, things are changing at a rate visible to most travelers. But, a few miles from the pavement, the lives of ranchers and villagers continue much as they have in previous decades.

Traveling by land means — for my needs — driving down in a high-clearance vehicle. This is necessary because I want to get into the backcountry. If you want to stay on the pavement and camp in hotels, you can drive down in any wreck whatsoever capable of making the journey. But I like to camp out and drive bad roads to mountain strongholds or remote coastlines (Mr. Krutch's notion of the symbiotic relationship between terrible roads and good places holds up today). For this, you need a rig with sufficient clearance off the ground so you won't rip out your oil pan. Four-wheel drive helps, but its absolute necessity is overrated. The gear-head mentality of associating Baja with dune buggies and Baja rigs tearing across pristine desert has encouraged a destructive glut of ATV recreational driving in northeastern Baja. ORV use devastates fragile desert communities. In terms of international

decorum, this industry is arguably the worst thing we export to Baja. One should never drive where there is not an existing track or roadway. Usually, when I am using four-wheel drive in the desert, I am driving where I should be walking.

I currently have a pickup and it is four-wheel drive. It has a camper shell to accommodate all my gear and water. I can also lock it up and leave it behind when I want to take off on a backpack trip or a visit to an island. I am invariably overloaded, so the suspension system is important; if it's not stiff enough you'll need to drive very slowly and gently over the rough spots. This is not a good place to break an axle.

94

An old international pickup and tables used for drying dates in San Ignacio.

San Ignacio.

Church and date palms at San Ignacio, a central Baja town west of Santa Rosalía.

San Ignacio.

On our first journey together down the Baja Peninsula, in the spring of 1972, Dr. Findley and I leased a vehicle for fifty dollars from a generous woman who indulged our cheap notions of travel. We promptly overloaded the borrowed International Scout with two thousand pounds of gear, including a six-man Avon inflatable draped over the roof rack and twenty-horsepower outboard in the back, along with a crush of collecting, diving, and camping gear. The spring assembly had so much weight on it that it flattened out over the axle like a collared lizard on a warm rock. I figured that I could gentle the overfreighted little rig over the graded or paved roads but was worried about Baja's notorious jeep trails. What we needed most were a few more spring leafs to give us a couple more inches of clearance.

Our port of entry into Baja was the border town of San Luis on the Colorado River. We pulled into the outdoor garage of a local mechanic, a little fenced yard with a small ramada roof as protection from rain and sun — a typical arrangement throughout arid Mexico. The mechanic thought it would be simple enough to stiffen up our vehicle, but he wanted to wait for his boss, the owner of the yard, who had the only car with which to drive around to the various junkyards and collect the spring leaves and other stuff we needed. The boss turned out to be a tall, handsome man who was living out a life in exile in this hot, dry place of refugees. His actual birthplace was

somewhat of a mystery, though no doubt far to the south, and he languished here in the desert, longing for the green fields and dark-skinned Nahuatl maidens of home. We toured the "Yunke" wrecking yards, finding the leaves but not the long-stemmed U-bolts with which to yoke them in place. For that we would have to wait for the automotive parts store to open in the morning.

The tall man sent out for *cerveza,* invited us to camp in his enclosure for the night, and took us under his care and into his confidence. Something had happened or he had perhaps done something terrible down south, causing him serious enemies and making it impossible for him to return home without being killed. His name was of no importance here in this city of *campesinos* and strangers. We set out on the town, tossing down shots of tequila, and soon heading toward the town's *la zona,* where our friend was well known by the regulars. He drew smiles from every woman with Aztec features, of whom there were many.

Outside the bar, from small restaurants with makeshift chairs and tables under outside ramadas, came the aroma of *nixtamal* — corn cooked with slaked lime, calcium hydroxide made from burned seashells from the Sea of Cortez, which softened the hull of the corn and allowed the kernel to splay into a white flower. They were preparing the hominy for *pozole,* the rich soup of pork and chiles that is weekend supper in much of southern Mexico. It was here the regional

origins of our tall friend could be discerned — if by then anyone still cared. The broth of the *pozole* was made by boiling a pig's head for eight hours. To this stew was added ground pumpkinseed, fresh tomatillos, and chile verde, making this a green *pozole* best eaten out of big earthen bowls and accompanied by mescal distilled from agaves found in the mountains of green Guerrero. The fragrance of mesquite from the open cooking fires blended with the pungency of chile, pork, *nixtamal,* oregano, and garlic. To this day, the smell of that street in San Luis lingers as a memory.

La Especial Café in Tijuana.

Years later, I still make my own *pozole* for special occasions, for food for the afterworld and at other times, and these cooking smells always draw me back into remembrance of places in Baja. The traditional pig's head is hard to find up here in the Gringo supermarkets, so I make do with baby pigs' feet with a pork shoulder tossed in. Canned hominy is easier, but lacks the texture and rich aroma of dried corn boiled in slaked lime.

When Ike Russell died, he was buried by friends and family in a place he loved. Ike was put in the ground with a Tarahumara bowl full of *pinole* (another native corn dish) to fuel his journey homeward. Likewise, Ed Abbey was laid to rest in defiance of laws concerning burial and embalming, carried by those who loved him deep into the desert, and planted with proper attention to food and drink for the hereafter. Each March I make an annual trip out to that spot, bearing little gifts, including a bottle of mescal and a bowl of *pozole verde*.

Baja is a great place to eat, whether you are eating in a little restaurant or cooking over a campfire. I prefer to haul along cooking gear and a few staples and otherwise live off the land and the local economy. The food of the region can be fabulous. I tend to eat what the locals do. It is best to keep an open mind; a Sunday breakfast for the *barrachos* (drunks) in Tecate of *menudo blanco* garnished with fresh oregano and chiletepin from the sierras. Fresh seafood anywhere: the abalone steaks in Guerrero Negro can't be beat, and I

97

The best taco stand in the world, Carbones, in Ensenada.

remember a filet of halibut *al mojo de ajo* in Lopez Mateos washed down with a bottle of vino blanco named after the queen of the Amazons — Calafia. When eating out, I tend to order what's made up or locally fresh. Don't worry if the cook sends someone out to buy ingredients; this means you're getting the freshest of the catch. Sometimes — if the restaurant is operating on a shoestring or if you're the first customer of the day — they might ask you to forward a bit of cash so they can go out and shop for your meal. Ask what's good or the special of the day, and don't be squeamish; I avoided missing out on an incredible meal of *tripas de leche* by taking such a tip. I could log my dozen or so trips down the peninsula by the memorable meals I was served or prepared.

The most important thing in the desert is water. Travelers generally buy distilled water for drinking at markets. If you are going to be out on the land, one of those filtration pumps is invaluable. These diatomite and other filter devices run from about forty to two hundred dollars. I have the bottom-drawer model and it is adequate for my needs: you can filter a half gallon of potable water from a goat wallow in five minutes. You can also use iodide or chloride tablets, though the cysts that cause amoebic dysentery are hard to kill and some people don't like the taste of chlorine or iodide at that strength. Even in the wilderness, you need to take care with your water; feral and domestic animals have penetrated nearly every last pocket. Rain from *tinajas* (natural tanks) or pocketwater with no animals is fine, but you must get there first. A knowledgeable friend informs me even birds such as mallards may transport giardia.

There is no reason to assume local well water is not potable, but since testing is uncommon in the backcountry you need to exercise some judgment. If the residents drink the water, usually so do I. This doesn't mean I am automatically immune to disease, because many intestinal afflictions associated with travel result from sensitivities to variants of *Escherichia coli*; one person's mountain spring water is another's poison. But a resistance to these strains of "turista" is quickly developed; most of these ailments are short-lived and more an inconvenience than anything else. The risk sometimes must be balanced against good manners in the backcountry.

I'm not saying there isn't a down side; in twenty-five years of Mexican travel I've had one severe intestinal disease complete with shaking chills and high fever. It hit me while driving the Pacific coast south of Todos Santos with my family. Suddenly I felt lightheaded, and my chest, shoulders, and arms began aching until my upper body was so tight I could hardly breathe. Knowing what was coming next (I suffered many bouts of malaria and other acute febrile diseases while serving in Southeast Asia), I had Lisa take over the wheel and head for the nearest beach. By the time we arrived at the ocean and struggled to erect a tent on a dune of yellow primrose and devil's club, I was shaking uncontrollably. The shaking chills lasted less than an hour; then my body temperature began to rise. When the fever hit 104 degrees Fahrenheit, the full complement of intestinal symptoms kicked in.

The kids were down by the seashore where a violent surf broke over the steep winter beach. We had warned them to stay well back of the water and they were behaving. A gray whale and her calf frolicked in the shallow water just yards off the beach. Beyond, in the setting sun, were spouts of more migrating whales. Lisa called Laurel and Colin back to the tent.

My little girl sensed the gravity of the moment and looked into my ashen face: "Are you going to die, Bappy?"

"I don't think so, sweetheart," I answered.

Outside the tent, sea lions barked and whales blew more spouts into the magenta of the Pacific sunset. It was a good day and a beautiful place to die.

One October I found myself killing time outside San Felipe. The desert near that coastal town is heavily damaged by trail bikes, dune buggies, and other versions of three- and four-wheelers. I have a grudge against these mindless vandals and didn't want to sit around nursing it. Instead, I spent the week extending my tentative explorations inland, around the

Blue and green palms near Santa Maria Mission.

eastern flank of the San Pedro Mártir, across the playas of the Valle San Felipe and Valle Trinidad, finally, to the foot of the Sierra de Juárez, the site of the only grizzly bear in Baja of record.

The human essence — as in most desert country — of this northernmost spine of Baja is water. The fresh water that tumbles, or trickles, down through palm canyons and the saltwater remnant, the playas, of the great inland seas. Excepting these dry lake beds — sizable terrain — and high tablelands of the sierras, the country is all up and down, with granitic ranges eroded into blocky outcrops and cut into sheer canyons.

Many of these canyons reach into the core of the north-trending sierras and have running water. The larger of these canyon oases, especially in the Sierra de Juárez, are lush and support groves of California and blue fan palms (*Washingtonia filifera* and *Brahea armata*). There are also a few cottonwoods and

some type of seep willow, perhaps *Baccharis salicfolia*. At any rate, it looks like the stuff near the Quitobaquito springs on the edge of the Cabeza Prieta.

These big valleys — Laguna Salada and Valle San Felipe — were probably created during the "spreading" of the ocean floor of the gulf more than five million years ago, in Pliocene and Pleistocene times. This is the same geologic process that created the Ballenas Channel, opening all these areas as saltwater basins. Salada has been mostly dry since the thirties; one report says it filled again in 1939, and again in 1983–1984. The process is no mystery: water from one delta distributary will silt up and another will find its way to the low ground. This cyclic flooding and drying was the way of the entire delta region before the coming of the white man. These shallow basins dry up in a season. Mullet accompany these periodic floods and are left behind, desiccating in the salt. After the 1922 flooding, Mexicans from Mexicali collected them for fertilizer.

Now, since the dams, only heavy flooding escapes the dams and the dikes and levees of irrigation. Laguna Salada belongs to that earlier era when the sea came and went in natural, irregular cycles. There are reports of the Spanish missionaries seeing the lake filled in 1771 and 1774. There is also a rumor of a wayward pirate schooner shoaled out and shipwrecked with black pearls aboard.

The Sierra de Juárez and San Pedro Mártir have the same look: a pale gray granite. Of course, they are extensions of the same mountain building system. San Matais Pass, between the Sierra de Juárez and the San Pedro Mártir mountains, is only a pass in the same cordillera; a low saddle studded with four-feet-high barrel cactus leaning southward among a garden of agave and cholla. The Juárez mountains are about four thousand feet in the northern end and six thousand feet near Laguna Hanson; Cerro Colorado itself is 6,677 feet high. The summit ridge is a rolling plateau, falling off to the east abruptly, to the west more gradually. A few small streams rise at the heads of gulches on the west. On the eastern front water is scarcer but occurs lower down in most of the large canyons.

I didn't find the area easy to get to; in fact, I was lost most of the way there. Again, the old travel guideline: anytime in Baja, one should budget much time to kill. The only map I had showed Laguna Salada in flood, which it was not. The easiest way in may have been from the top, the western approach. But from the east, access is from one of many dirt tracks leading through the fossil dunes on the shore of old Laguna Maquata, now called Laguna Salada. You end up doing more driving up smoke tree washes than I care to; accordingly, I bushwhacked the last couple miles, aiming about four or five canyons north of what I imagined to be Agua Caliente canyon. If you don't

have a lot of time, this is not a very good way to get into the country.

By the time I reached the foot of the sierra, the sun had begun its decline in the west. Though I imagined the canyon an unnamed one — since I wasn't sure which one it was — I crossed jeep tracks any number of times. There were broken grinding stones and a few Venus shells in the dunes. I aimed for the south fork, a branching canyon. That was all the time I had.

The country, as is most of Baja, was overgrazed, though I saw no cattle. Inside the mouth of the canyon were boulders, which precluded jeep travel. Shortly thereafter, native palm trees — the northernmost I had seen in Baja. The canyon narrowed and pockets of damp sand lay among the boulders. On the walls were dim petroglyphs of abstract designs carved into the decomposing granite. There were two kinds of fan palms which I assumed were the California fan palm and the blue fan palm.

Many white-winged doves were present, and mourning doves called from farther up the canyon. The year was dry but, had I proceeded up the arroyo, the call of the mourning dove ("Whooo Cooks for Yoooo") told me I would find water.

And in the desert, that is everything.

101

Hills at the entrance to Cañón de Guadalupe, in the Sierra de Juárez, on the west side of Laguna Salada.

> *". . . each rock and shrub and tree, each flower, each stem of grass, diverse and separate, vividly isolate, yet joined each to every other in a unity which generously includes me and my solitude as well."*
>
> Edward Abbey

I would be the last to rag anyone for having studied poorly during high school Spanish class. But, even if you only wish to camp out away from people in remote areas, your range of activities and access to the secrets of the land and the wealth of wisdom from those who have lived there the longest is necessarily limited without knowing the language. My advice is to carry down an English/Spanish dictionary and brief yourself on four or five words relevant to the next situation for which you will need some Spanish; four words for a seafood dinner, four for visiting cave paintings, where to see birds or find the marshes and esteros, and so on. Keep it painless, and remember that local information in Baja — especially about natural history — can reflect bias as often as it does wisdom.

When traveling the backcountry, I like to live off the land as much as possible. Gathering is a delightfully natural way of learning about the land. I try to balance what I take with common sense, local practice, and good manners: I don't hunt in Baja, and if birds need the fruit or berries I don't pick them. I enjoy this subsistence activity everywhere I go, learning little Native American secrets about plants and sea life up and down the continent. Baja is indeed a plant gatherers' special challenge. When Euell Gibbons of *Gathering the Wild Asparagus* fame went down the peninsula with his students to live off the land, they almost starved to death. But the Baja region can also be an incredibly rich — if seasonally fickle — place to gather your own food. The key to success is to listen to the wisdom of the native people who lived there.

Although much of the archaeology and ethnology of Baja is unknown, the utilization of local plant foods can be inferred and otherwise guessed at from the natural history of the peninsula and knowledge of other native peoples of the desert. As many as eighty species of plants stood between the people and starvation, and even more kinds were used for medicinal and ceremonial purposes. Beyond these vegetable foods, there was the animal kingdom on the land and, more diversely, in the sea. A seasonality linked everything together.

Central desert south of Calamajúe Canyon.

Sunrise, Cañón de Guadalupe.

Major plant-food groups were cactus fruit, especially *Pitahaya dulce*, agave hearts, seeds from desert trees like mesquite and paloverde, and, in the upper gulf region, plants such as eelgrass and salt grass.

Agave were harvested in January and February, sometimes a bit later depending on the elevation and species, at the end of the brief winter. These century plants — many different species but especially several species in the subgenus *Agave* — provided an important sugar source during an otherwise lean season. The plant was harvested just before it threw up a gigantic stalk. An agave about to flower grows progressively narrower and smaller leaves in the middle. The concentration of carbohydrates allows the plant to shoot up an enormous inflorescence in a very short time period. Droughts negatively affect flowering. Plants were pried up, the leaves trimmed back to the white core, and these hearts roasted in pits overnight. Raw agave is caustic and dangerous and must be cooked.

Agave plant, near Desengaño.

During the last stages of its life, the coastal agave shoots up a magnificent bloom and then dies,
sometimes turning unique shades of red, orange, yellow, and green.

About April, in the upper Gulf of California, thousands of pounds of salt grass, *Distichlis palmeri* — a drought-resistant halophyte, washed up on every tide and the Cucapá collected it from windrows. Farther south, by Tiburón Island, Seri Indians gathered ripe eelgrass, *Zostera marina*, as it floated in as mats. The seeds of both are harvested.

In early summer the columnar cactus fruit and bean pods of mesquite and paloverde ripen just before the summer rains, timing their seeds to the fertility of the monsoon. Cactus fruit can be sun-dried by slicing the ripe fruit and spooning out the sweet pulp to dry for several days. The seeds of the trees were — as were many other seeds and plant foods — toasted, then ground in metates, and used as flour or gruel.

Suddenly, in midsummer, monsoons transform the desert into a green garden; spadefoot toads miraculously appear in every puddle, the land is renewed and, by August, plant food is everywhere. It is a good time to travel. In the central Baja Peninsula, there are few areas, even coastal, that could support more than a few humans year round; people had to move around, making rapid forays to the coast for shellfish or elsewhere for other foods, taking advantage of the weather, traveling after rains when *tinajas* and potholes were full.

In practice, I don't gather these plant foods that often. I have harvested each food group at one time or another. After all, full-time gathering is time consuming and sometimes I'd rather just lay back and eat out of a frijole can. But living off the land is a wonderful way to enter a regional ethnobotany: an autumn day hiking up a foothills wash picking chiletepins under wolfberry, the tiny red pear of chiletepin catching your eye as it grew up through hummingbird bush and brittlebush, *Encelia farinosa*, like tiny lights on a desert Christmas tree.

Roasting agave hearts is something I try about once a decade. The first time I didn't roast the heart long enough — it was one of those big zebra agaves from Seri country — and it was bitter, and like biting mouthfuls of pulverized glass. The last time, I did four ripe hearts from the slopes of San Pedro Mártir by the book: dig a pit about a yard on a side and a couple feet deep, line the hole with rocks, torch a huge fire of oak and mesquite until the red embers begin to turn white, place the mescal hearts in the center, pack them with hot rocks and a foot of dirt, then go to sleep. The next morning the agave was shrunk and charred black. Inside, the center was like yam, though not as soft, the color like a dark sweet potato, and the taste surprisingly sweet (one of the hearts was markedly sweeter than the others).

Yucca and prickly pear in the Sierra de Juárez above Cañón Agua Caliente.

Cardon with moon.

Cactus fruit is simple to collect. The important ones are *Pitahaya dulce* and *Pitahaya ágria*, cardon, and, on the Sonoran side of the gulf, saguaro cactus. You knock the ripe fruit from the tops of the arms with a long pole, or, in the case of the organ pipe — the most productive of fruiting cactus — from alongside the arms.

One year I had to live with grizzly bears in the far north and I wanted a backpackable food that grizzlies wouldn't be attracted to or familiar with. So I harvested and dried about fifty pounds of saguaro cactus fruit, figuring that knowledge of saguaro cactus would not live in the genetic memories of grizzlies. The only place in the American West where bears didn't live was in the low deserts. I tied together enough columnar cactus ribs to knock the fruit off the thirty-foot-high plants. The fruit was ripe when the green skin showed just a blush of crimson. Wary of external spines, I split the egg-shaped fruit open and spooned out the red pulp loaded with tiny black seeds onto a screen. I covered the screen with another to keep the flies off and set it out in the late June sun for three or four days, until the dried fruit was the consistency of chewy taffy. The grizzly-proof food testing is still ongoing; so far, so good.

Of all the foods I carry into the wilderness, tsampa is my staple. I prepare tsampa with chiletepin and *Distichlis*. The chiles I pick myself but salt grass (also called wild wheat) is hard to find in the wild thanks to the dams on the upper Colorado and irrigation projects downstream. In fact, in 1982, *Distichlis palmeri* was declared extinct. I had seen salt grass growing on the north end of Angel de la Guarda and way up the gulf on the Sonoran side but never very much of it and never when it was fully fruited. So I buy cultivated wild wheat (available through NyPa, Inc., 727 N. 9th Ave., Tucson, AZ 85705) from this Tucson couple who see salt grass as a way to feed the hungry of the world by growing the salt-resistant *Distichlis* in saline soils irrigated with seawater. Besides its messianic qualities, salt grass is a tasty little grain, low in sodium, nutritionally superior to wheat in several ways, and high enough in fiber — beware! — that one should never eat it straight.

Tsampa, Tibetan in origin, is mixed grains, roasted and cracked. I was introduced to it by Yvon Chouinard, who said: "You can eat it day after day, and never get sick of it." This endorsement, from a man who has taken more serious expeditions to eight-thousand-meter mountains than I have to the beer store, impressed me. Yvon's stateside version of tsampa is made from multiple-grain cereal, and I have modified it slightly adding native seeds. You soak the dry cereal for fifteen minutes, then dry it by roasting in an oven or over heat in a heavy pot with a tablespoon of olive oil, stirring constantly. I grind chiletepin I have picked myself in an ancient metate and add about a teaspoon of flakes per quart of tsampa. I toast a quarter cup of *Distichlis* in a small amount of oil or butter for a few minutes in a skillet until it pops, and mix the wild wheat in with the tsampa for bran and texture. Like granola, the homemade version is always better.

Traveling on the water is a pleasure all its own, and the sea is one of the most practical paths to the magic of the wild desert coast. The only large boat I've spent time on off Baja is the *Don José* out of La Paz. Beyond what you can both pick up and paddle, I'm no sailor. But kayaking and inflatable rafting are also great ways to move up and down the coasts from drive-in points. A rivermate of mine from the Arctic Wildlife Refuge has canoed much of Baja's coasts — both, but especially the gulf side — simply taking enough time to have the luxury of wisely abiding by the weather. On good days he would paddle in the morning as long as the ocean chop held back until he reached another decent camp. My buddy carried water but wasn't particular when it came to food. He carried a meat grinder and a box of spices. Each day fish, lizards, sea gulls, crickets, and many less savory creatures disappeared into it. The man traveled for six weeks at a time like this.

If you are traveling with anything you can carry — like yourself and a backpack, a small raft, or a sea kayak — you can hire a fisherman to drop you off at a great base camp. This is one of the best ways to visit coastal Baja. The price of passage depends on how the fisherman is doing and how busy he is. One fisherman at Old Kino in Sonora told us he normally earned a thousand dollars a day fishing. We passed on his services. Another day spent out of Libertad on an Easter weekend to watch fin whales was twenty-five dollars for the *panga*, four Gringo biologist-types, three fishermen who didn't have much to do, and the captain. We paid for the gas. These coastal or island interludes are good deals if you like being off by yourself. If you carry a kayak with you (a fisherman's *panga* can easily accommodate a sea kayak), your mobility is greatly enhanced.

The first chance that came along for me to be on a desert island with a sea kayak was only a couple of years ago. An organization of river-running fanatics had recently screwed me out of $206 at a time when I was dead broke. They got me to buy a nonreturnable round-trip ticket in order to give a lecture at their annual convention, then — while I was out of the country on Tiburón Island in the Sea of Cortez — found someone else to replace me. Without explanation, they refused to reimburse me. Naturally, I put them on my list of bad guys to get even with.

It was about May before I got around to putting my full attention and all my talents into repaying these river swine. Since they claimed to be some kind of conservation group and got most of their operating expenses from environmental

Puerto Balandra, north of La Paz.

Pedro MacLesh, who came to work at El Mármol in 1945 and is still quarrying onyx there with his sons.

and charitable foundations, I decided to hit them where it hurt the most — in the pocketbook. So I bad-mouthed these double-dealers far and wide, up and down the environmental grapevine. I caused these people a lot of trouble, and, by summer, the scumbags were feeling the pinch.

The red, fifteen-foot sea kayak arrived by an unmarked freight truck. The vehicle was owned by a fly-by-night delivery outfit that wanted an extra twenty-two bucks, which Lisa paid on the spot, and which, subsequently, proved a nonremovable blemish on her credit record and the usual nightmare of accounting gobbledygook. The receipt said the river people had shipped the kayak. I knew signing it meant the peace would be made and I would have to stop bad-mouthing the river people. I scrawled my name on the paper.

But it wasn't over yet. The craft itself had a giant dent across the bottom, as if it had been flung from the roof rack of a VW bus and wrapped itself around a cedar tree. At any rate, the beat-up kayak spoke silently of tragedy and bad karma. A gaping hole in the hull was sealed with a foot-wide patch glued with a clear substance I now imagined to be saltwater soluble. On the top of the stern were stenciled two numbers: "1" and "3."

I was understandably apprehensive about field testing my little kamikaze kayak, and it was December before I was finally dropped off by a fisherman on a big spit of land overlooking a mangrove estero miles from the nearest human on the southwestern Baja coast. I didn't want anyone watching in case I messed up. I had been glib in pretending I knew all about these suckers when in fact I had never seen the inside of a sea kayak. I

The onyx school house built in 1927 at the quarry at El Mármol.

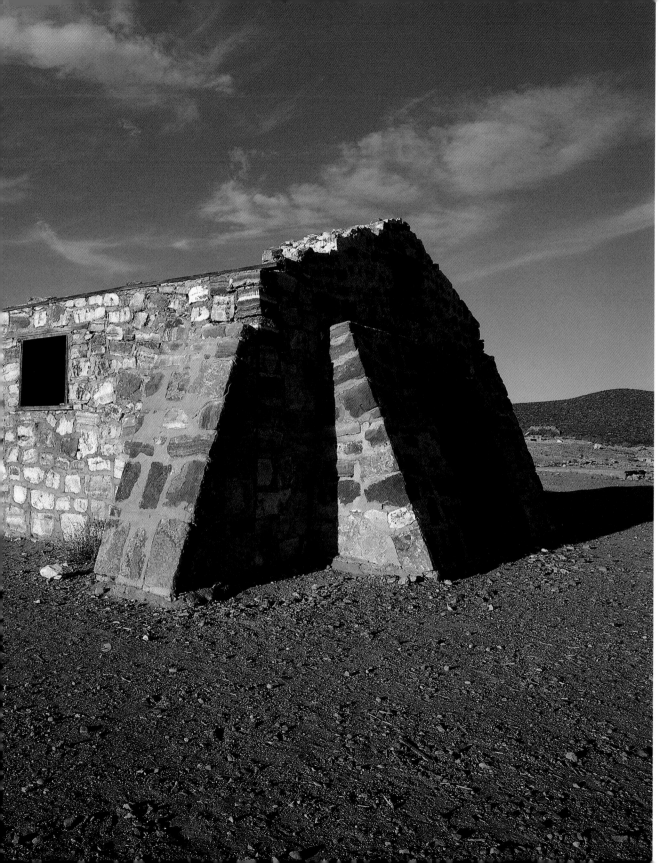

hadn't even gotten around to reading the book I'd brought along, *The Coastal Kayaker's Manual.*

I placed old number thirteen, *"número trece,"* as I called it, along the shore of the quiet lagoon. The tide was going out, and across the channel green-backed and black-crowned night herons roosted in black mangroves; a quarter mile to the south, an emerging finger of sand was covered by two colonies of big white birds — white pelicans and white ibis. Here and there were rafts of brant geese in the quieter water. The soft silt of the estero fell off steeply, but the water was less than a foot deep where the kayak floated. I took my time pushing the craft out a few feet so I could wash the bottom muck off my sandals. I found I could steady the kayak with both hands behind me on either side of the cockpit. I eased my left leg into the opening and down into the bow. Straining, with all my weight on my hands, I rinsed the dirt off my right foot and lifted my leg over the bow and into the kayak. Now I was floating. I lowered my entire large body down onto the seat.

The next thing I knew I was upside down with my head buried in the bottomless muck of the estuary. I tried pushing off the bottom with my hands, but the slime was so soft I couldn't get any leverage. I tried falling off to the side, but my legs were stuck in the kayak, which was floating on top of me, holding me down. The water was only a few inches deep here, but that fact is of little consolation when your head is stuck in the ocean bottom.

111

The only thing I could think was that those river bastards had planned this.

I gasped for air and sucked in a mouthful of silt. My eyes were blinded by the mud. With all my strength I kicked upward, lifting the sea kayak into the air. I kicked again and somehow freed one leg from the mouth of the giant red banana that was suffocating me. The last kick sent *"número trece"* flying, and I fell over on my stomach in the filthy water, pulling free my arms and head, which came out of the muck with an enormous sucking sound.

Later that day, I turned to chapter 9 and mastered — in a graceless sort of way — the launching of the kayak. My exact location was in the northern reaches of Coyote Bay south of Cresciente Island. Though I worried every second of several hours that first day about the dissolving patch, nothing happened. In the next two days I explored dozens of miles of mangrove channels by kayak, logging five kinds of herons, cattle, common and snowy egrets, and once catching a glimpse of a clapper rail. I would pull *"número trece"* out on a sandbar at low tide and tie on a silver and blue number 2 anchovy fly on the end of my daughter's sporting number 5 Cortland graphite. Corvina were the most fun to catch on the fly rod; they ran in the swift channels of the dropping tide. When you caught one, there were always more. I didn't catch many corvina, but often two or three, one after the other. I also caught bonefish, croaker, and, using weighted wooly buggers, halibut in the mangroves.

113

Blocks of onyx, El Mármol.

The most abundant food fish was, however, the cabrilla de roca, which, if fishing near the bottom, you could catch on every other cast.

Sometimes the focus of your travel and your curiosity is triggered by a written image. This certainly was the case reading the literate phrases of Joseph Wood Krutch writing about fossil ammonites in *The Forgotten Peninsula*:

Despite its inaccessibility, these fossils were discovered quite a few years ago and specimens collected there have been distributed to many American museums. The country is hilly and in a small valley cut by an arroyo, the surface is strewn with what look like enormous snail shells curled in one plane, much like the "red snails" of the home aquarium, but several feet in diameter.

And then the phrase that so captured my imagination, ". . . so numerous as to make one think of the elephant graveyards of legend." I knew that these fossil shells had been long since carried off by a variety of collectors, but the image of an "elephant graveyard" was reason enough to go have a look.

The place was called Santa Catarina Landing after the port from which the onyx mined at El Mármol, forty-five miles to the east, was shipped until the bottom fell out of the onyx market when plastic inkstands replaced the finely veined sedimentary stone on desk tops everywhere.

Boojums.

This area is about a fourth of the way down the peninsula in the northern part of the Central Desert where the upside-down carrotlike *cirio* or boojum trees grow. I had driven down with my friend Mitch and his dog Lou. Our trip had a less than auspicious beginning out of Tucson when Lou got into a bowl of Lucky Charms left out by my son, Colin, and had thrown up the colorful cereal on the front seat of the car twenty minutes into our Baja adventure. Minutes later, Mitch, known for a notoriously weak stomach, also upchucked — perhaps sympathetically — head out the window, down the side of the vehicle.

By now, some five hundred miles into our journey, the smells of sickness had faded. As we neared the Pacific, the road dropped off a dissected plateau onto a playa cut by a large sandy wash — the place where Krutch had seen all the ammonite fossils. Down on the flat the vegetation thinned out; only a few elephant trees, cardon, pitahaya, and *cirios* grew along the arroyo to within a mile of the ocean, but of course the area was overgrazed by livestock. The village of Catarina was, like El Mármol, nearly deserted. Three houses were occupied by relatives of the same family who made most of their living fishing for spiny lobster.

Mitch's Spanish was at an all-time low; in the throes of a tequila hangover his mind was a pig sty. The people said, he thought, that there hadn't been any *caracoles* or ammonites for "*muchos años.*" Which meant collectors had carried off Krutch's elephant graveyard many years ago. But I knew there was a whole mountain of these big fossils a couple of miles up the arroyo; we had hiked up there and found countless fragments of ammonites still imbedded in the sedimentary rock. We'd even picked up a few large sections of fossilized chambered nautilus someone had left behind at a camp decades ago. We didn't care; this was the place and we were here.

We made camp in a dune behind the rocky beach near the south end of the bay. In the sand were flakes of chert and obsidian, hammerstones and grinding stones of basalt and dacite amid the shells of clams, scallops, and oysters. Above us, on the rim of a mesa, were petroglyphs pecked into brown patinas on the jointing surface of a basaltic flow. Most were curvilinear abstractions, but there were at least two figures with outstretched arms. Out on the sea, lines of brown pelicans soared along the breaking waves, gliding to evening roosts. The sun was setting and the tide dropping, so we headed to the beach to look for something to eat.

115

A marker with flotsam and jetsam on Malarrimo beach southwest of Guerrero Negro on the Pacific coast.

Blue mussels clung to boulders everywhere, but I was interested in finding some clams. We dug among the rocks and coarse sand with screwdrivers, digging peck-size holes into the lower beach. The sea was an average winter rough, but the offshore slabs of basalt broke the force of the waves as they spilled and rolled over the shelves. We groped blindly for the cherrystone — actually a small *Tivela* — clams at the bottom of our ten-inch-deep pits; the little Venus bivalves were so common we had an easy bucketful in half an hour. I rinsed the little cherrystones between two buckets then set them aside in a pail of clean water to give them time to purge more silt from their digestive systems. Meanwhile, we set up tents against the heavy Pacific dew. I moved a bark scorpion, which had crawled out of the firewood, to a new home. Though very small, *Centruroides sculpturatus* packed a nasty sting, as I knew from firsthand experience.

Sunset at Cabo Falso, Pacific coast.

The sun dropped into the heavy atmosphere of the western Pacific. I collected more firewood from the upper dune while Mitch and Lou combed the beach for driftwood. By dusk the fire was roaring and I had a skillet going with Mexican butter, a large white onion, and a head of garlic. I parboiled potatoes in a backpacking kettle at the same time. When I could stick a filleting knife into the spuds, I removed them and drained all but an inch of water. I added clams to the brim and covered the steaming pot with the lid, which I weighted down with a large grinding stone from the beach midden. As soon as the clams steamed open, I plucked them out, eventually adding more and repeating the process until I had a pile of steamers. We scraped the clams from their shells with our Swiss army knives. I gradually added canned milk, blending it into the sautéed garlic and onion, then added the diced potatoes, a small fistful of ground hot red chile, a half glass of vino blanco, a sprig of fresh dill, salt and pepper, and the juice of four limes — all the time stirring and keeping the temperature well below boiling to avoid the inevitable curdling of boiling acidic milk and butter. We added the clams and heated up the whole thing to just below a simmer until the diced potatoes were *al dente*. Lou got a can of dog food from me because I like dogs at least as well as I do many people. The dew was sopping, so I built up the fire to keep the moisture at bay. We ate the chowder in front of a roaring blaze of driftwood with the din of Pacific surf shouting in our ears.

117

Camping the desert is the most effortless of outdoor activities. It doesn't matter if it's out of your kayak, your pickup, or backpack; there is nothing in our modern world quite so accessibly primordial.

Though it would be foolish to argue that the desert is the best of all places to live — the unrelenting summer heat, the unending preoccupation with finding water — there is something about the desert. And there are times — times of year, times of life — when I would care to be nowhere else. I am not a desert rat of the extremes and caliber of hard-core friends like Ed Abbey. I generally migrate seasonally to the mountains of the Northern Rockies or the tundra of the far north five or so months of each year. Even so, I figure I have spent a third of my life in the desert where I was not born.

Perhaps it is simply in the ease of living outdoors, those totally benign winter days with an abundance of the world's best firewood, which burns long into the night, the coals lingering until daylight. The vistas are gigantic, the solace of openness to myopics and claustrophobics such as myself, a leap of eye and mind capable of pulling me out of the darkest melancholy in minutes.

And, even today, simply driving along a desert highway, my vision is drawn up washes and arroyos, looking for habitat, human habitat, because in every bend of dry riverbed, under the shade of paloverde and ironwood is a place for me to live — for months if necessary — a place to make an evening bedroll under the skies, stoke an acacia-wood fire long into the dark skies filled with stars seen nowhere less arid, and lingering into late morning watching the bluest of skies beyond crisp distant desert ranges, finally lounging in the shade of the trees in the midday sun.

Baja California is a comfortable, easy place to camp. Although I have camped over a hundred nights out of bases supplied by boat and vehicle, the great untapped Baja resource (for me) is to roam unfettered, living out of a backpack, exploring the remote interior of the peninsula, climbing over a volcanic pass studded with pitahaya, and looking down another unexplored wild palm canyon. I haven't traveled nearly enough this way. In twenty years, these are the trips I dreamed of taking but only sampled on two memorable but short-lived expeditions.

On the other hand, these unfulfilled dreams suffice. As long as the enchanted wild backcountry of Baja is there, the possibility of dreaming oneself into this lovely landscape lives on. We don't ever have to go there, as long as we could if we wanted to badly enough. I hope I do, of course. Either way, the unconsummated journey — this leap of imagination — will accompany me to the grave.

All one needs is time.

"After a short climb we emerged on a level place in a deep cleft in the granite mountains. In this cleft a tiny stream of water fell hundreds of feet from pool to pool. There were palm trees and wild grapevines and large ferns, and the water was cool and sweet."

John Steinbeck

Stream and ferns in Canon del Diablo in the Sierra San Pedro Martir.

Fog over Sierra San Borja.

the central desert

Siempreviva plant.

Boulders near Cataviña.

Barrel cactus with flowers.

Boojum, ocotillo, and cardon.
Boojum grow only in the Central Desert between
El Rosario in the northwest to just north of Santa Rosalia
to the southeast, and in one spot along the gulf coast
in Sonora. Boojums are so well adapted to arid
climates that in a very dry year, they may not
grow at all. In a very wet year, they can
grow as much as seven inches.

Cochal cactus in flower
near El Arco.

Cardon and boulders, near Cataviña.

124

Brittlebush flowering
near Mezquital.

Desert lavender.

California poppies, east of Ensenada.

"The wind will not stop. Gusts of sand swirl before me, stinging my face. But there is still too much to see and marvel at, the world very much alive in the bright light and wind, exultant with the fever of spring, the delight of morning."

Edward Abbey

**"Strange growths
of a strange land!
Heat, drouth, and
starvation gnawing
at their vitals month
in and month out;
and yet how
determined to live,
how determined
to fulfill their
destiny!"**

John C. Van Dyke

126

Barrel cactus, detail.

Boojum and cardon
near Cataviña.

Cardon.

"What, then, is this astonishing tree like?
The right answer is 'like nothing else on earth,'
though the commonest description is
'like an upsidedown carrot improbably provided
with slender, spiny, and unusually leafless
branches which seem to be stuck
helter-skelter into the tapering,
carroty body.' "

John Wood Krutch

Flowers of the barrel cactus, detail.

Boojum trees.

129

Sunset from Rancho San José de Meling on the western slope of Sierra San Pedro Mártir.

A pioneer ranching family —
Andrew Meling and his sister, Aida, with her grandchildren,
Tim and Sonia. Founded in 1907 by hardy Scandinavian
immigrants, the Meling Ranch was originally a cattle ranch,
but has lodged guests for more than forty years.

Shrine of La Virgen
north of Rancho Santa Inez,
Central Desert.

132

Pictograph cave near Cataviña.

Desert pavement south of Laguna San Ignacio near the Pacific coast.

"The dry sand, scattered with pebbles, seemed alive. The surface of the ground was palpitating softly, steadily, as if breathing. And each pebble, formerly so dull and sunbleached, now shone like a jewel."

Edward Abbey

A mummified cow, Rancho Santa Inez.

a trip across the peninsula

I first took my children, Laurel, who is eight, and Colin, six, to Baja in late winter of 1990. Laurel had previously visited the gulf islands and La Paz as a toddler. Colin, though a frequent visitor to Sonora, had never been across the gulf.

With their mother, Lisa, Peter Matthiessen, and myself, we trucked down from Tucson to catch the morning ferry from Guaymas to Santa Rosalía. In previous years these ferry rides (between Guaymas and Santa Rosalía, La Paz and Topolobampo, La Paz and Mazatlán, and sometimes Cabo San Lucas and Puerto Vallarta) were one of the great deals of Mexican travel, despite the harassment of minor bureaucracy and bribery. You could get yourself, your vehicle, and your gear over to the Baja Peninsula for about twenty bucks. The better ferries were almost luxurious, with staterooms, good food, and fifty-cent margaritas to be sipped on deck while looking out into the sunset at sounding fin whales. This past year the fares were drastically escalated (with no decrease in the attendant hassles), and now the above package costs anywhere from about a hundred bucks to two hundred and fifty, depending on the particular route and your class of travel.

Our little tribe boarded the ferry just before 8 A.M. and departed shortly after. The morning easterly breeze created a false hope the ride would be hastened by a tailwind. Up north we could see the heavy bank of clouds we had escaped the day before, driving down from Tucson in record time. We cleared Punta Narizon and San Antonio and locked into a south-southwest bearing for Santa Rosalía. The tiny island of San Pedro Nolasco, thirteen miles up the coast, came into view as we navigated out of the harbor and out into the open sea. Though San Pedro Nolasco lies only eight miles off the mainland of Sonora, the vegetation is highly distinctive and contains a high percentage of endemic species, especially the cacti, showing isolation.

On the western horizon a cloud of diving birds came into focus; the swarm of pelicans, boobies, gulls, and terns was directly in the path of our ferry. As we approached the feeding birds, we could see the water froth below them; something was driving up baitfish from below. Now we could see the dorsal fins of hundreds of common dolphins who were perhaps feeding on jacks or mackerels in turn slicing through the enormous school of sardines.

135

Dolphins feeding, Gulf of California.

Aerial view of San Lorenzo Island, Gulf of California.

The feeding was over by the time we got close enough to see what kinds of fishes were on hand. The dolphins broke away from the feeding frenzy and began racing alongside the ferry, diving in synchronous arcs just off the bow and portside where we were watching. There were so many dolphins — the school numbered perhaps a thousand — that they seemed to me uncharacteristically small. Yet they were unmistakably *Delphinus delphis,* distinguished by a narrow dark band around their eyes extending out to the corner of the narrow beak and yellow-brown stripes on their sides, so the average size must have been five or six feet in length. The size of this school was as large as any I had seen in the Gulf of California. They rolled and leaped, following the ship for a mile and a half. We felt our lives had been blessed.

A midday chop picked up as the dominate westerlies reasserted themselves. I stayed on deck glassing the horizon for spouts. Laurel, Colin, and Lisa went below. In past trips to this part of the gulf I had spotted fin and a few gray whales along with a single immature blue. Dr. Findley had told me to keep an eye out for pygmy sperm whales, *Kogia breviceps,* especially as we neared Tortuga Island, which lay eighteen miles northeast of Santa Rosalía. My instructions were to look for "cedar logs" floating heavily in the waves, with a small dorsal fin behind midback and a bulbous head. Total length would be nine to

136

Graveyard, Santa Rosalía.

twelve feet. The pygmy sperm whales that had been sighted here previously were "basking" on the surface or swimming slowly with very short surface dives. Though these are toothed whales whose larger cousin, *Physeter macrocephalus* — the sperm whale — dines regularly on giant squids, the pygmy sperm of the gulf feeds on smaller squids and brown shrimp.

This time the whale watching doesn't pan out. We pass Tortuga in a stiff breeze with the sun sinking toward the Sierra Guadalupe. The island is a dark basaltic moonscape with just a hint of erosion tracing the beginning of arroyos down the outer slopes of an emerging volcanic crater. Tortuga, along with Rasa Island, is the product of recent activity; the surface craters are Holocene as contrasted with most of the other gulf islands, which are Pleistocene in age and have resulted from geologic block faulting, uplifting, or emergence in the Sea of Cortez.

It was sunset by the time the Guaymas ferry reached the breakwater marking the tiny man-made harbor at Santa Rosalía. Instead of pulling into the mooring, the ship steamed up the coast a short distance and dieseled in circles for three more hours before docking. There were rumors the harbor master — who was the only one who could give permission to dock — was out for dinner or perhaps drunk. But in fact the full moon — signaling a big low tide — had risen behind us and this port is said to be one of the poorest on the peninsula. The

Model A Ford, Santa Rosalía.
Until the late 1940s the Model A was the most common car in Baja.

Mexican passengers took the delay in stride and in good humor; one can learn from people who are kind and patient toward children. We felt fortunate after a Santa Rosalía woman who had befriended us told us that the same ferry had once circled just offshore for forty hours before dispatching its passengers and cargo.

137

Brown pelican in flight.

That evening Lisa, the children, Peter, and I blasted south along the coast, finally making camp among the cardon and palo blancos of a coarse wash draining the Sierra de Guadalupe. We wanted to be poised for a strike into the mountains the next morning to visit a painted cave. I kindled a small fire with dried brittlebush and creosote while the others bedded down in their sleeping bags. I wanted to gentle myself into the country a bit after the relative crush of humanity aboard the ferry. In the distance a truck noisily geared down a steep hill and groaned up the next ravine. The quiet eased back in and I heard a distant owl — perhaps a screech. I poured two fingers of tequila Sauza in a tin cup, and turning in, tossed an ironwood stick on the fire.

The next morning we packed up and headed south toward Mulegé. There was a cave I wanted the kids to see on the way down; it was one I had previously visited years ago during the monsoon season. It was one of the southernmost sites of the great murals, a cave site called Cueva San Borjitas. We found the turnoff and followed the dirt road into the Sierra de Guadalupe. Leaving the pickup behind, Peter, Laurel, Colin, Lisa, and I hiked up the canyon. Though the place has long been known, we saw no one on our hour-long hike in.

The great cave astonished us all. My daughter's impression confirmed my own suspicion of years ago: "The people painted on the ceiling with their arms out and five or six arrows going through them, well, it was like a burial ground."

She wondered about the great size and height of the paintings, "how they got up there, because they're high up; did they have ladders?" I told her the Indians said the men on the ceiling were painted by Giants.

At the back of the cave, carved in the soft volcanic rock, were little vaginas. My children, especially Laurel, were interested in this practice. The basic representation of the vulvas — and these by far are the most abundant here at San Borjitas, as well as at countless other sites in Baja and throughout North America — is a circle or horseshoe open at the bottom encompassing a vertical line or slit. These are thought to be symbols to aid fertility of game or tribe, though elsewhere — among modern Pueblo Indians in New Mexico, for instance — they are calendars or records by individual women marking the time of their puberty. At any rate, these petroglyphs of vaginas also occur in the southeastern tip of Baja, at Bahía Coyote, and at numerous caves in the central sierra as well as other places. These symbols are recorded worldwide, throughout the prehistoric record: as petroglyphs from the late Paleolithic period in southern France, from British Columbia painted in red ocher, and, two thousand years ago, pecked in limestone near St. Louis, Missouri.

Later that day, we drove down the coast Indian-pickup style: Lisa, Laurel and Colin in the back, Peter and I in the front. We picked up Yvon Chouinard at the airport in Loreto, adding him to the front seat.

The next stop was kid paradise: a beachfront sand dune with no cactus or, this time of year, rattlesnakes. We hired a friend of mine, a fisherman named Salvador, to take us out to this island in his *panga*. We were joined by the Budniks and the Moores. The island doesn't have a name and it is really only an island in the most transitory way: it is a mobile spit of beach dune twelve miles long and a mile and a half across. It is largely barren of vegetation, with only a few halophytes and perennials like lupine and penstemon on the upper dunes, and the thin line of mangroves hugging the lee of the dune — and these are continually invaded and buried by drifting sand.

We all set up our tents on the dune. Laurel, who has been camping since she was born, decided she would sleep alone in her own tent with only her stuffed duck. This was a first. Each morning, she was up at dawn, as she never has been before or since in Tucson, walking down the dune by herself, passing Peter's tent. "Good morning, Peter," Laurel would say with a smile, and drop off the dune to fish the channel for cabrilla.

There was nothing here to draw anyone but local fishermen, nothing except whales. The area a few miles south of our camp was a popular place to watch gray whales. We liked whales too, but didn't come all this way just to hang out with other Gringos.

The place was great for watching birds. With the help of Mitch, Peter, and Lisa, I came up with about seventy-one species for this small but diverse area. The outer

Gulf coastline near Bahía Calamajué.

coast is visited by arctic loons, grebes, cormorants, red-breasted mergansers, forester's tern, and seven species of gull. Black-bellied, Wilson's, semipalmated, and showy plovers, sanderlings, curlews, yellowlegs, avocets, oystercatchers, whimbrels, marbled godwits, willets, ruddy turnstones, long-billed dowitchers, and sandpipers chase the tongue of wave up and down the flat shingle of the Pacific Ocean. Inside the dune, rafts of brant geese, pintails, mallards, and American widgeon floated on the calmer waters of the estero. From the mangrove-lined channels came the call of belted kingfishers and mangrove warblers. Overhead soared turkey vultures and ospreys, while inland, in the salt scrub and, beyond, among the desert scrub vegetation, flitted and roosted doves, wrens, hummingbirds, owls, quails, flycatchers, and phainopeplas.

The children's favorite activity was finding live sand dollars. Across the dune, to the west, rolled a great flat beach; the waves broke far out and gently spilled in — as safe a Pacific beach in Baja for children as any. "There were lots of old shipwrecks and whale skeletons," recalls Colin. It was also the best beachcombing I had ever seen. There were perhaps two dozen conspicuous shelled species of clams, oysters, and scallops, plus a huge whelk and another big white gastropod — *Malea ringens.* But nothing compared to finding live sand dollars. The sign on the sand at lowest tides was "like a cat track; we could dig them up with our toes; it was so easy,"

said Laurel. Indeed, once you identified the first sign, the sand dollars were a common delight.

Our food staple was cabrilla de roca or *hamburguesa del mar* (hamburger of the sea), as I called them. "They're stupid and aggressive," said Yvon, and I had to agree they were easy enough to catch. As Colin put it: "My friend Yvon, he caught a fish every cast. It was so great!"

We got them on every variety of white and yellow feather streamer stripped in, not too fast, along the silty bottom of the mangroves. When the tides were high and running, you could hook cabrilla, corvina and bonefish almost every cast up into the roots of the black mangrove. Mostly, we fly fished, even my children. Everything worked. Peter caught a small halibut on a white jig in front of camp; it was too small to fillet but we cooked it anyway — *al mojo de ajo* — in olive oil with lots of garlic. This is not exactly sport fishing; dinner is usually foremost on the mind.

One gray morning I watched a huge flock of brown pelicans dive and feed on a school of baitfish out in the roughest part of the *boca.* The dive-bombing

Young pelicans.

went on for a very long time, and by midafternoon they were still at it. Yvon had been watching them too.

"Let's go see what's pushing up those baitfish," he said.

I rounded up Terry, who got the Zodiac ready. Yvon and I grabbed our fly rods. We motored out into the channel of the estuary and into the mouth — the *boca* — where the Pacific pushed through into the mangroves. The tide was running high and the wind was up. The heavy surf of the open ocean rolled into the *boca* and collided with the tide. The wind-generated waves combined with these, and at the eye of all these forces was a slick of water the size of a baseball infield and this little flat of sea was surrounded by the most fierce chop in the entire *boca* — strong enough to flip the fourteen-foot inflatable in a second. This was where the pelicans were diving, and had been diving — one of the more sustained pelican feeding frenzies I had seen.

By the time we hit the middle of the *boca,* it was clear we were a bit over our heads; not Yvon, with his death-defying kayak adventures, but the pilot and myself as navigator might have been somewhat out of our element. Yvon was up in the bow with fly rod poised. We didn't know what to expect under the half beaks, sardines, anchovies, or whatever the hell was providing the giant ball of bait — maybe jacks or bonito. There were bigger ones in the channel; gray whales rolled and sounded, sometimes within a few yards of our raft. In all, perhaps a dozen grays moved in and out of the *boca.*

Waves of sand cover a dune island at Bahía Magdalena.

California gull.

We crested a hundred yards of brutal chop and entered the eye of calm water. The sky had darkened toward late afternoon, but I had no idea what time it was. I screamed at Terry to turn as a giant wave rolled over the slick. Brown pelicans dove everywhere; they ignored us — as if we were nothing. The birds dove on fish a foot from the Zodiac. A gray whale rolled forty yards out in the channel. Yvon was now casting, sideways and low over the waves to escape the wind, and behind him a score of pelicans were diving and sitting on the little flat, beyond the raging surf and dark Pacific sky. I paused a half second to appreciate the gravity of this spectacle of nature. I yelled again and Terry turned away from the chop, which on three sides was strong enough to capsize the little boat. Yvon hooked something. I couldn't wait any longer and stripped out line and whipped a silver anchovy fly into the surf. A fish struck and for a moment we both had fish on. Yvon boated the fish; it was a beautiful jack smelt with blue gills, about ten inches. Yvon wanted something bigger but jack smelt is all we got — about eight of them.

We lived, and back at camp Yvon prepared sushimi of jack smelt.

141

a river no more: the colorado river and the islands of the gulf of california

For millennia, the channel of the Colorado River alternated its flow between the northern basin and the open gulf. During the periods when the river dumped into the basin, creating Lake Cahuilla and other prehistoric lakes, it probably drained into the Sea of Cortez via the Río Hardy. More recently, the course of the Colorado shifted back to the present channel where it remained until the arrival of Western man and his irrigation projects. These operations resulted in the accidental filling of the Salton Sea, at which time the river was rediverted back into its original course.

The average annual flow of the Colorado into the gulf was over fifteen million acre-feet at the turn of the last century and the amount of sediment dumped each year was estimated at over forty million tons. The effects of the Colorado pouring into the gulf could be seen as far south as La Paz.

As late as 1922, Aldo Leopold found the Colorado River delta "a place of green lagoons, lovely groves and awesome jungles where the jaguar still prowls." Long before, it was a garden of Eden for the Cucapá, who hunted its richness and gathered wild wheat off the beaches from windrows left at high tide.

In 1905 the course of the Colorado was diverted and in 1935 the Hoover Dam was completed. The river ceased flowing while the reservoir behind Hoover Dam was filled. Since then, the river was tamed with more dams, including Glenn Canyon, a man-made reservoir which drowned two hundred miles of unparalleled canyons — a man-made outrage visible from space. No river in the world is used so much by humans: every drop of Colorado River water is utilized three times before being returned to the lower river, and, by this time, the water is probably loaded with pesticides and fertilizers (the data are inconclusive and even contradictory here). Ninety percent of the water is used to grow hay to feed cattle, which constitute a mere four percent of the national beef market. Below Yuma is a soggy marsh, the last gasp of the poisoned Colorado River, where ibis and the endangered Yuma clapper rail live.

Today the flow of the Colorado River at the delta is normally a trickle, and sedimentation has virtually ceased. What little water reaches the upper gulf flows mainly underground, then via the Río Hardy, and that fresh water is polluted by agricultural pesticides, fertilizers, and human sewage. The lack of flow means less DDT, which might mean more osprey and brown pelicans; the other side of the equation is that the lack of sediment from the river results in less nutrients in the gulf waters, and this is a negative of such magnitude that its consequences can only be guessed.

143

The Río Hardy, the principal channel of the Colorado River, not far from where it reaches the gulf. Unless the river is in flood, the water in the Río Hardy comes from agricultural drainage from the Mexicali Valley and tides that push seawater up the river from the head of the gulf.

A Cucupá Indian family who fish the Río Hardy.

Late afternoon along the Río Hardy with Sierra de las Cucapás in the distance.

The story of the *vaquita* is evocative of much of the last decades of history in the region: it is the tale of a modern species of animal that humans nearly pushed into extinction before they noticed it existed.

The first scientific recognition of the Gulf of California harbor porpoise came in 1956 after biologist Kenneth Norris found a bleached skull on the beach near San Felipe in northern Baja. He and a colleague studied the skull and realized they had discovered a new species of porpoise, *Phocaena sinus,* whose closest relative was thought to be Burmeister's porpoise found off the southwestern coast of South America some three thousand miles to the south. Local fishermen, who knew about the little porpoise all along, called it *vaquita* — the little cow.

No further reports of *P. sinus* were received until the mid-1960s, when U.S. Fish and Wildlife marine mammalogist Robert Brownell, Jr. collected a number of partial skeletons from upper gulf beaches. Later, Lloyd Findley, then a graduate student at the University of Arizona, heard of Brownell's search and remembered a photograph taken by a fellow graduate student, Christine Flanagan, of a dead female and her calf killed in a gill net set for totoaba, and another picture shot by Don Thomson of a dead animal also entangled in a gill net and discarded at a garbage dump outside El Golfo de Santa Clara. He passed the photos on to Brownell, who notified Norris: *vaquitas* were threatened by the proliferation of gill net fishing in the upper gulf.

Little further research was undertaken until 1975, when Bernardo Villa of the National University in Mexico City began to survey *vaquitas;* he saw very few porpoises but so many gill nets he concluded the *vaquita* could be close to extinction and included the Gulf of California harbor porpoise on a list of endangered and rare Mexican species.

On a similar list was a huge corvina-like croaker or weakfish, the totoaba. I remember first seeing a commercial catch of these big fish at San Felipe in the early 1970s on a trip down Baja with Findley. But by 1975, the totoaba catch had plummeted to one-fortieth of the peak-year harvest and the Mexican Ministry of Fisheries, Pesca, banned further taking of totoaba. Though no protective measures were taken on behalf of the *vaquita,* it was hoped the moratorium on totoaba fishing would also help spare the porpoise.

The problem with the ban on totoaba fishing — which is still in effect today — is that its enforcement has no teeth; the moratorium was only loosely enforced, if at all. At present there are more totoaba, shrimp, and shark fishermen working the upper gulf than ever before. One San Felipe source, whose reliability is unknown, said about eight hundred boats — meaning *pangas,* trawlers, and others — were illegally harvesting juvenile shrimp and totoaba in the northern gulf. Another eyewitness, researcher Omar Vidal, estimated the illegal totoaba catch at fifty metric tons (for a three-month

period) and most of this was exported through Mexicali into the U.S. market as "sea bass." Much of the catch is juvenile totoaba in the eleven- to twelve-inch range sometimes caught in three-and-a-half-inch mesh gill nets set for Sierra mackerel and corvinas. Floating two-inch gill nets are especially effective because of the immense tidal range in the upper gulf; these nets are designed for shrimp but work well on totoaba. Shrimp trawlers pull in huge catches; Mexican biologists Juan Carlos Baonera and Gerardo Polo once estimated that about ninety percent — and perhaps as much as ninety-five percent — of all totoaba of any year class were removed by trawlers. If that were not enough, there has been a fad market created around foods produced from manta rays, sting rays, and smaller sharks and there are hundreds of gill nets, some sixty leagues long, often crisscrossing the upper Sea of Cortez. The great tides rush out leaving up to five miles of exposed flats with balls and remnants of gill nets everywhere; the nets don't go away and the nylon doesn't rot.

Tidal mud flats along the Río Hardy.

Vaquitas, who are regarded by the fishermen as just another trash fish that could rip up the valuable nets, die in all of these. Alejandro Robles, who had studied with Findley and Vidal, retrieved seven *vaquitas* drowned in several nets in a single spring morning in 1985. Shortly later, he obtained six more fresh carcasses from fishermen and eventually hauled all thirteen to the lab near Guaymas that Vidal and Findley supervised. All these are from a single population whose lower limits have been estimated at one hundred to three hundred animals.

The Gulf of California harbor porpoise has the most limited distribution of any cetacean on earth. It is being driven into extinction as a result of "incidental mortality" in fishing operations that are mostly illegal. The people who study the *vaquita* are good people who care about both the porpoises and the fishermen who accidentally kill them. The local fishermen, especially the *panga* fleet, have been living in a marginal economy with few occupational choices. The 1975 ban left few alternatives to a black market; fishing was subsidized and ambitious catch goals were set, with no idea of the size of the fish populations. Researchers are sympathetic to these men skilled in a worthy trade they know to be on the way out. In the short run life is good; the market is holding and there is relative prosperity.

Today the principal researchers working in the northern gulf are largely out of the Instituto Tecnologico de Estudios Superiores de Monterrey campus at Guaymas, and the Centro Ecologica in Hermosillo, Sonora. They include, coincidentally, my friends Findley and Vidal.

In the fishing villages of the northern gulf, there is unaccustomed affluence; you see new four-wheel-drive pickups in nearly every yard. There is also, reports one of the scientists, recreational cocaine use for the first time in anyone's memory. What makes life easy is a fishery that is often targeted on protected species.

This is not to say that Mexico is plowing under her marine resources; though virtually all parties agree that gulf fishing is on the decline, there is very little hard data. The sardine catch — a traditional index since these little fish are near the bottom of the fish food chain — is down. But Mexicans are not the only fishermen out there, and the biggest fishing boats are not flying Mexican flags.

Squid are also an indicator of sorts. Off Santa Rosalía and Guaymas, "licensed" foreign ships netted school after school of large squid until, in 1981, they were gone. Local protests led to a moratorium on foreign squid factory ships, but their permits were renewed the year after. Professor Vidal told me a more recent violation of a "collecting permit" involving squid: fourteen miles north of Santa Rosalía a Korean ship was boarded and inspected. Their only permit to be in these waters was one of the

"collecting" types, an expensive piece of paper bought from corrupt officials in order to undertake dubious scientific endeavors. The hold of the factory ship was full of frozen illegal squid. This permit was one of eighty-one such "collecting" permits granted for the area.

In early April of 1989, the jumbo squid were back. Whether this return is more related to natural cycles than to curtailing fishing is unknown. Giant squid in the gulf up to fifty feet, have been reported, though eighteen to twenty-four inches is more common. Dr. Findley and I once saw a six-footer washed on a beach of the island of Angel de la Guarda. Squid are ferocious predators, often schooling up and hitting baitfish. They are a favorite food of toothed whales, including dolphins and sea lions.

Sedimentation from the Colorado River also supplied nutrients for the marine life off the islands of the Sea of Cortez, the big islands of Angel de la Guarda and Tiburón in particular, where the tidal flows and upwellings became more prominent in deeper waters. Again, the magnitude and subsequent loss of fertility from the Colorado can only be guessed at. But these islands have a character and a magic all their own.

Islands are not for everyone, and the fifty-five or so islands off Baja's Pacific coast and in the Gulf of California certainly don't need any more attention than they're already getting. Although I

Pepe Smith, a fisherman, Bahia de los Angeles.

have lived over a month on Angel de la Guarda, Santa Catalina, and Tiburón, these places are hard to get to and are stark, bone-dry landscapes, barren and rocky. I don't recommend going there.

But I was raised on a diet of *Treasure Island* and *Robinson Crusoe* and cannot shake these images from my dreams: the shape-shifting of the floating white clouds at sunrise; the billowy shores covered with barking sea lions. Or kayaking the mangrove tunnels of the southern tip of Isla San José, pargo exploding in the shallows, me seeking the elusive mangrove warbler whose trill carries across the narrow waterways. My first spiny lobster, in four feet of water off Santa Catalina, was so big that the powerful kicks of its tail jerked my entire body as I tried to swim off with it.

Dr. Findley and I spent nearly three weeks on islands, visiting a half dozen but living on only two. The first of these was the big island of Angel. We had to do a lot of diving and I knew next to nothing of scuba techniques. There was no time for formal training; Findley briefed me as best he could, and my maiden dive served to sweep out the bottom of the swimming pool at our going-away party in Tucson.

The second descent was for real off the north end of Angel de la Guarda, my first solo dive. It was two hours before slack tide, and I packed up my diving gear and hiked north through the halophytes and scabrous vegetation over a low pass to the very northern tip of the main island. A few torote trees and creosote bushes overlooked a boiling channel about two hundred fifty yards wide and flowing west to east. Beyond was the smaller Mejía Island and two rocky islets occupied by roosting seabirds and small colonies of cardon. One of these headlands had brown pelicans nesting on the top, a peregrine eyrie and Craveri's murrelets on the side, and fishing bats (*Pizonyx vivesi*) living in the cracks and caves. I avoided the rock because the pelicans were extremely spooky and abandoned their nests if disturbed, so I never approached closer than about five hundred yards.

I scrambled down to a tiny beach and pulled on my borrowed wetsuit and flippers, then waded out backward into the channel until I was almost waist deep. I squatted and the current knocked me off my feet and swept me eastward toward a rocky headland. I was surprised by the strength of the spring tidal bore. The water temperature seemed several degrees colder than other gulf water of similar latitudes. I turned around and swam toward the setting sun, kicking against the tides with sufficient effort both to maintain a stationary position and generate enough body heat to stay warm. Clouds of upwelling plankton and small debris, along with a few fish, drifted by as I hovered behind a large rock, finally ambushing a small dinner-size cabrilla with the Hawaiian sling.

This persistent pool of cold water along the west side of Angel de la Guarda Island is the most conspicuous thermal structure in the Gulf of California. Infrared pictures taken from satellites in 1980 revealed that the Ballenas Channel, the Channel of the Whales, is the coolest surface water of the Sea of Cortez. The rest of the gulf reflects seasonal patterns of temperatures driven by winds and tides. This gigantic static pool alongside Angel de la Guarda Island is unaffected by winds and is probably the result of strong tidal mixing in the deep Channel of the Whales. These same satellite images showed cold plumes of water propelled before the strong winds of spring. This was the most evident during this same first week of April, when upwellings were the strongest.

A shrine built by fishermen on Mejía Island.

A California sea lion with her pup.

Alcatraz Island, Gulf of California.

Baby blue-footed boobies under a cardon.

Adolescent brown booby, San Jorge Island.

Nesting caspian and elegant terns on Raza Island.

A tropic bird above San Pedro Mártir Island.

There does seem something different, altogether wilder about this island. Though the spine of the island is a single chain of volcanic flows, tuffs, and sandstones overlying older metamorphics and you can inspect nearly all the surface topography from the deck of a circumnavigating boat, the interior looms impenetrable and unknowable. There are deep hidden arroyos draining the Cerro Angel on the north end of the island and large palm canyons on the eastern midsection. There is rumored to be no water, though in fact there are large tanks on this central eastern slope, one of them in the northernmost of the palm canyons big enough to swim in (though it is poor desert manners to swim in another's drinking water) and never dry in any but years of total drought, which are not unknown on this arid island. The decaying volcanic rock is so rotten and treacherous that slopes steeper than forty degrees are largely unapproachable. Yet if you scramble up the volcanic talus on the northeast side of the collection of summits which constitute the Cerro Angel, you can see colonies of stunted boojum trees clinging to the highest slopes. Angel de la Guarda is said always to have been uninhabited, although on *bajadas* west of Punta Rocosa there are flakes and scrapers of dacite and obsidian and mysterious circles of rocks on a ridgeline leading back toward the head of one of the larger palm canyons.

153

"Like so much of the peninsula, it is cut by deep valleys running down to the sea where they end in sheltered coves, many of them enclosing white sandy beaches irresistibly inviting."

Joseph Wood Krutch

Cove, Espíritu Santo.

Fish camp on Espíritu Santo.

Espíritu Santo Island, north of La Paz.

Among all the islands of the gulf, Tiburón stands apart; it is the biggest in area (467 square miles) and has — by a huge margin — the most drinking water, which makes it livable. Over three hundred species of vascular plants (570 species of plants have been identified on all the islands) live here, and the island has the largest numbers of big mammals, especially deer and sheep, which have in part allowed for perhaps eight thousand years of human occupation.

Of course, you don't see the relative fecundity of this arid landscape right off. What you see first from across the straits of the "little hell" is one of the ruggedest, bleakest, driest, hottest wastelands of the lower Sonoran Desert. You see the jagged outline of the Sierra Kunkaak and peaks of the Sierra Menor beyond, never suspecting the great interior valley lying between the two — a broad playa studded with cardon and pitahaya, home to the densest population of mule deer remaining in the cactus forests of Sonora and Arizona. The valley was also home to the last Seri Indian band to come in from the wilderness.

Nobody knows how much rain falls on Tiburón; it isn't much. The west coast gets more than does the Infernillo Strait twenty miles to the east. Some years it may not rain at all. The average is probably four or five inches per year and comes mostly during summer monsoons and occasional tropical *chubascos*.

I didn't get a chance to visit Tiburón until February of 1989, just before Ed Abbey died, and the trip was taken with his health very much in mind, as I intended to be with him at the end. I picked up my friends Rick Ridgeway, Claire, Fletcher, and Yvon Chouinard at the Tucson airport, and we drove down together to Kino Bay, where Mitch Wyss was waiting for us. We crossed the Infernillo Strait before the morning chop blew up, passed Datil, and arrived off the southern tip of Tiburón Island at midday of February 18.

We passed a gray whale and her calf halfway through the Infernillo, which was very far north for such a sighting. From

Cardon in flower, with Tiburón Island in the distance.

"The blooms, each two or three inches across, are creamy white with a cool green cast and thick waxy petals. All pop out of the south side of the stalk in the most unlikely way, as if stuck on like doorknobs. The flowers are pollinated by bats, which, in the evening, arc from luminous flower to luminous flower."

Ann Zwinger

156

Cholluda Island with Tiburón Island in the distance.

Iguana, San Esteban Island.

Yellow chuckwalla, San Esteban Island.

the headland above our camp we could see spouts of fin whales far out in the morning calm. Orcas were also resident but, at that time, I had never seen one. Though I had been within a mile of orca pods a dozen times, I seemed always to have been looking the other way.

The interior of Tiburón is one of the great delights of the lower regions of the Sonoran Desert. All four large columnar cactus grow here: senita, saguaro, organpipe, and cardon or sahueso — the largest cactus in the world. The plant communities are unaltered by domestic livestock grazing and support more mule deer than any other desert area I have visited. The island also teems with jackrabbits, coyotes, and rodents. Bighorn sheep were introduced between 1975 and 1987, and one recent count put the number at fifty-two individuals. Javelina, white-tailed deer, and antelope are not found and this may explain why so many mule deer live on the island. Also, big predators — mountain lion and jaguar — are missing, though I found a set of small cat-tracks off the southern coast.

We set up our base in a tiny, protected cove off the southern tip of Tiburón, unloading our sea kayaks and other camping gear from the fisherman's *panga*. Beyond the pebbly beach, a lovely white wash climbed gently into the interior. Paloverde and a few ironwood trees provided shaded campsites and, upslope, yellow brittlebush covered the south-facing rocky hillside. Noisy mockingbirds, perhaps mimicking cactus wrens, called from the limberbush

thickets. Costa's hummingbirds buzzed the red blossoms of ocotillo and hummingbirdbush.

One morning we were all occupied with our various duties; Claire was collecting seashells, Fletcher was diving for turban snails for dinner, Mitch was birding, Yvon was fishing, and I was inland trying to identify some weed. Rick, like Yvon a world-class climber, was naturally climbing up the vertical face of the granodiorite headland. Rick paused halfway up the face. Above him, a peregrine falcon complained loudly. He

looked back down; thirty yards out from the foot of the cliff was a big flat rock. On either side of the rock, a killer whale paused, facing in. From the ocean side, two-thirds out of the water, rose a huge male orca, landing on top of the flat rock, eyes rolling from side to side, looking for sea lions. Rick said the encounter was "the quintessence of his animal experience in life so far."

At that very moment, naturally, I was pondering the genus of my weed, impervious to the singing of the fabled orca.

Brown pelicans.

Giant barrel cactus, which can reach twelve feet in height.

the pacific coast whales

The natural history of the gray whale, like that of many large mammals, begins with the impressions of those who nearly succeeded in hounding or hunting the animals into extinction. This body of literature, such as Scammon's logs, is not inconsiderable. So-called serious scientific research began only about twenty years ago. By that time the population had so recovered that today it is estimated that the numbers of gray whales is at or above the 1850 historical level of about eighteen thousand.

Gray whales are baleen whales, like blues or humpbacks, and lack the teeth of sperm or killer whales. Two populations — the Korean stock and California stock — live in the Pacific and number perhaps twenty thousand. In the North Atlantic, the gray whale is extinct. They are of medium size: thirty-five to forty-seven feet for males, and a couple feet longer for females. Their mottled gray color comes from barnacles and whale lice attached to the skin.

Gray whales are gregarious and they like shallow water, so they are highly visible from land. Pacific Northwest coastal Indians hunted from great whaling canoes burned out of giant red cedar logs. Other traditional gray whaling industries operated off the Siberian coast and the Bering Sea.

160

A young gray whale in Laguna San Ignacio on the Pacific coast.

Subsistence hunting by native peoples with traditional technology had little impact on the gray whale population. For that, we wait for the nineteenth century, about 1840, when European and American whalers hunted the west coast of Baja. Captain Scammon was the most famous of these. He was apparently the first outsider to find, in 1857, the narrow mouth into an unsuspected lagoon where enormous numbers of gray whales gathered during the winter months. The story goes that rival whalers, astonished by the speed with which his ships filled their hulls with whale oil and returned to San Francisco, followed Scammon, spotted his smoke rising from behind a dune, and, investigating, discovered the lagoon. These and other ships joined in the slaughter.

Captain Scammon was a keen observer who went on to publish a work on marine mammals, which contributed to the preservation of several species of animals he and his men helped drive to the brink of extinction (these two edges of the same enthusiasm are often linked). Scammon and his men were aware of the beauty and charm of this desert country and the awesome and picturesque spectacle of the whales: his logbooks show this. But the bottom line was immediate profit, and the business was necessarily a bloody one. The most dramatic and discussed strategy was called "whaling among the breakers," which alludes to the taking of whales at the mouths of bays or otherwise in the shallows where mothers sheltered their calves.

It appears to be their habit to get into the shallowest inland waters when their cubs are young. . . . Sometimes the calf is fastened to instead of the cow. In such instances the mother may have been an old frequenter of the ground, and been before chased, and perhaps have suffered from a previous attack, so that she is far more difficult to capture, staving the boats and escaping after receiving repeated wounds. One instance occurred in Magdalena Lagoon, in 1857, where, after several boats had been staved, they bearing near the beach, the men in those remaining afloat managed to pick up their swimming comrades, and, in the meantime, to run the line to the shore, hauling the calf in to as shallow water as would float the dam, she keeping near her troubled young one, giving the gunner a good chance for a shot with his bomb-gun from the beach. A similar circumstance instance occurred in Scammon's Lagoon in 1859.

His 1860/61 logbook records the scene:

Here the objects of pursuit were found in large numbers, and here the scene of slaughter was exceedingly picturesque and unusually exciting, especially on a calm morning, when the mirage would transform not only the boats and their crews into fantastic imagery, but the whales, as they sent forth their towering spouts of aqueous vapor, frequently tinted with blood, would appear greatly distorted. . . . Numbers of them will be fast to whales at the same time, and the stricken animals, in their efforts to escape, can be seen darting in every direction through the water, or breaching

162

headlong clear of its surface, coming down with a splash that sends columns of foam in every direction, and with a rattling report that can be heard beyond the surrounding shores. The men in boats shout and yell, or converse in vehement strains, using a variety of lingo, from the Portuguese of the Western Islands to the Kanaka of Oceania. In fact, the whole spectacle is beyond description, for it is one continually changing aquatic battle scene.

In 1937, gray whales were, in theory, protected from commercial whaling. The first sanctuaries in the world for whales were established by Mexico in 1972: Laguna Ojo de Liebre and Laguna Guerrero Negro. Later, the calving grounds of Laguna San Ignacio and Magdalena Bay were added.

Every autumn, gray whales leave their feeding grounds in the Bering Sea and migrate five thousand miles to these bays and lagoons of Baja to mate and calve. The route normally closely follows the coast, though there have been recent cases where migrating gray whales looped far out to sea along the California coast. A few whales continue on around Cabo San Lucas to remote bays along the Sonoran coast, although this number is now very small. Research by Mexican biologists, including Lloyd Findley and Omar Vidal, indicates the Sonoran population of grays was considerably larger in previous decades, and these scientists believe the decline in the number of mothers with calves is related to motorized boat traffic in these once-remote areas.

Today, two observations concerning gray whales collide: that, among all the whales, grays have the most affinity for shallow water and traveling the coasts, and that they are also sensitive to disturbance, even seemingly benign intrusions, such as the motors of fishermen and whale-watchers, whose engine frequencies may mimic the complex language of whales.

Whale-watching as an industry is probably as innocuous as anything to hit Baja California, but there is something about our notions of recreation that always merits examination. For example, the aspect of trekking to a remote and sparsely populated part of the world in order to stand elbow to elbow with a score or more of your ethnic peers in an intrusion on a species who didn't ask to be so closely watched while they make love and give birth. After all, these animals make the longest migration of any mammal to accommodate these biological necessities. One cannot ponder the evolutionary realities that drove this extreme journey without noting that the cold waters they feed in in the north are as remote from the intrusions of modern man as any and that the warm lagoons of Baja were also — until a heartbeat of recent time — equally distanced from the disturbing activities of humans.

The whale-watching industry suffered its biggest potential setback in the winter of 1989/90, when the gray whales failed to return to Scammon's Lagoon. There were newspaper accounts and speculations that the *Exxon Valdez* oil spill had somehow done the whales in, since gray whales feed in the Arctic and many pass through the region of Prince William Sound on their annual migration southward. Dr. Findley wondered if anyone had measured the depth at the entrance to the lagoon to see if the bar had become too shallow. Or did the reason whales avoided the place have something to do with what the grays were encountering inside Scammon's? A member of the 1990 Interspecies Communication *Beluga* expedition pondered about the collective and genetic memories of whales: did these twentieth-century cetaceans somehow hear the ancient screams of harpooned calves and mothers slaughtered in the 1850s?

163

Gray whale spy hopping.

A gray whale covered with barnacles.

164

Salt formations on
the Estero de San José
near Guerrero Negro,
on the Pacific coast
just north of
Scammon's Lagoon.

Later, I heard, they did show up. The question of whale sensitivity to humans, the magnitudes and types of activities, remains. Jim Nollman, of Interspecies Communication, who literally designs, plays, and broadcasts underwater music for killer whales off Vancouver Island in British Columbia, noted that, of the hundred-some orcas in the area, only two were interested in what he had to say. He, of course, is talking about communicating with animals. The point is those receptive were a tiny percent of the population; many more steered clear than came in. The same percentages might apply to the populations of gray whales that are currently so valued for their "friendly" encounters — that, for every whale that solicits the attention of biologist or tourist, a hundred more might be swimming away.

Off the coast of Maui in the Hawaiian Islands, researchers have testified that increased boat traffic, particularly thrill craft, have had an impact on humpback whales, causing mothers with calves to abandon their critical near-shore resting areas. Omar Vidal and Lloyd Findley have expressed similar suspicions concerning the abandonment of historic gray whale calving grounds in northern Sinaloa and Sonora: that the sheer weight of outboard motors — the endless drone — at some point becomes more than the whales will comfortably endure.

Perhaps we are killing the goose laying the golden egg, that the whale-watching industry — with all its benign baggage of low-impact intentions and whale-touching sensitivities — has driven off the object of their watch with too many motors. This is an imprecise area of science; the jury will always be out in a laboratory as big as the ocean, where many factors impact whale demographics. Like other intelligent mammals, whales may become habituated to predictable disturbances that the animals learn hold no threat of harm to them. It is necessary to distinguish these minor annoyances from real threats to these sensitive species. Although there are other factors to explain the gray whale's habits, it seems wise — especially in the case of rare animals subject to human-induced population fluctuations — to take a conservative approach and cut back on our disturbing activities.

One night I camped at the head of a wild *boca* twenty-five miles south of San Ignacio National Park. I had camped with others three miles away across a spit of dune and wanted to get off by myself for a night. I crossed the dune two hours before sunset and hiked up the shell-littered beach barefooted, finally dumping my Kelty pack in the low dunes just as the sun began to dip into the ocean. On the walk up I had watched the spouts of perhaps fifteen or twenty whales mostly cruising south parallel to the beach, but now one of them came halfway out of the water just outside the mouth of the bay. I hurriedly threw up my tent to ward off the heavy dew of the Pacific. Out to sea, I could see the approaching fog bank. Plovers, godwits, curlews, but mostly sandpipers chased the surf, running up and down the gentle beach. The big gray whale breached again, rising twenty feet out of the sea and collapsing with a great splash just feet from my tent. Farther out another whale breached. Some of this could have been "spy hopping," which whales may do to look around for navigational landmarks. The big whale in front of my camp breached twice more, rocking her thirty-five tons into the inner bay. Just as the sun dipped below the horizon, the heads of three more whales rose out of the sea, apparently heading into the calmer waters of the estero for the evening. The wind picked up, speeding the arrival of the heavy bank of fog. I retreated to my tent. Through the roar of the pounding surf, I heard one last blow and puff from a whale not fifty feet away. As the fog settled in, I looked up through the billowing mist and out to the east; the waning moon, dimly lit, rose out of the desert.

I have been blessed with having met many whales off the coast of Baja and around the islands of the gulf. The first were fin whales off Angel de la Guarda on my thirtieth birthday, a day when the gulf was still as glass and the Sierra Seri visible from the hills of Baja above Bahía de los Angeles. Years later, I saw a young blue, then many grays, even humpbacks and minke whales, and finally the elusive orca. I have yet to encounter Bryde's, pygmy sperm, or its larger cousin — but I know they are out there somewhere. The presence of whales is always unexpected to me, a gift, something cosmic, a titan world traveler who always reminds me to open my mind and expand my insular journeys.

Flukes of a diving whale.

A gray whale blowing.

A baby gray whale.

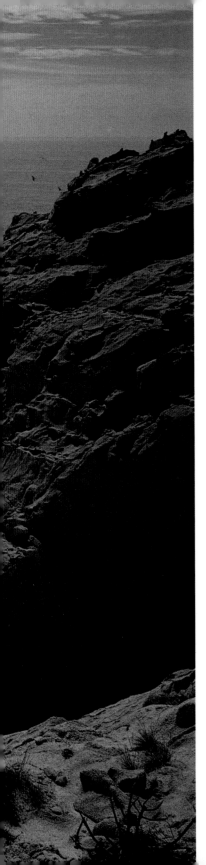

future of the baja region

A blowup of an old photograph hangs on the basement wall of the Evolutionary Biology building at the University of Arizona. The picture shows an immense froth of water the size of several football fields just off the beach of the upper Gulf of California. It is a feeding frenzy featuring a giant school of Gulf croaker, now thought to be extinct, who are driving a school of baitfish right up onto the beach. The scene is one of great power such as I might imagine a photograph from the high plains in 1800 when a flock of passenger pigeons would block out the sun for three days or a herd of six million bison would stain the sand hills of Nebraska black.

This comparison of the northern Sea of Cortez with nineteenth-century Nebraska (or Kansas, Missouri, or the Dakotas) sticks in my mind. The upper gulf is such a fertile marine region, supporting impressive numbers of fish, invertebrates, and marine mammals. Yet this bioregion is a shadow of its former richness when great schools of Gulf croaker, yellow-fin corvina, *vaquita,* and totoaba cruised the flats. The upper gulf may be like the Nebraska of 1860 or 1870; the high plains of the American West still supported ten million bison preyed upon by packs of wolves while grizzlies roamed the cottonwood bottomlands. That landscape seemed so wild and rich that people believed it would last forever. By 1881, however, they were all gone — all the buffalo, grizzlies, and wolves, along with the great swarms of passenger pigeons and countless smaller animals. The subsequent plowing under of the fertile prairie grasses sealed forever the fate of the American High Plains fauna.

The situation in the Sea of Cortez is more optimistic than the wheat fields of Nebraska. The northern gulf will not be plowed under; the habitat will remain, and so long as the quality of the habitat is unchanged, the decline of the marine resources can be turned around. Yet local fishermen and researchers alike speak of the end of fishing in a decade or two. The take from the current level of gill netting and trawling cannot continue and still sustain a renewable resource. Everyone agrees on this. Shortly after the turn of the twenty-first century, the great shrimp, totoaba, shark, and ray fishery may be, like nineteenth-century Nebraska, just a memory. We might have only the photographs.

169

Cabo San Lucas, looking southeast at the tip.

In the Pacific, the indicators that might show us the relative health of the marine fishery resources are harder to find than in the gulf. It is, after all, a very big place. Before 1950, the Mexican sardine fleet operated out of Ensenada. Increased harvests of California Current sardines led to a population collapse in the late 1940s. That fishery now operates out of Guaymas, and there is fear that overfishing in the gulf will precipitate a similar crash in the Sea of Cortez. A short, annual moratorium on sardine fishing was declared in 1987 for the summer months, but none for the winter spawning period. Pacific sardines are a barometer of sorts, near the base of a food chain which supports not only all kinds of fish and marine mammals but also the three hundred thousand Heermann's gulls and another seventy thousand elegant and royal terns which nest on nearby Raza Island in the Midriff Islands in the Gulf of California. Along the Pacific coast of Baja California Sur, the sport fishing associated with the mangrove bays and esteros has suffered in predictable ways: pargo and snook are much depleted or fished out where gill netting is common.

Frigate bird, Cabo Falso.

But it isn't until one reaches the cape region that one hears the loud complaints of the Mexican sport fishing industry. Long-bill species, especially marlin, are the focus of much of the tourism business in southern Baja. The complaint, that foreign long-liners flying Japanese flags steal in by night to plunder billfish, has been documented a number of times in the past decade. In May 1982, the *Fukuju 17*, a Japanese boat flying the Mexican flag, put into Cabo San Lucas. A "surprise" inspection revealed a hold full of frozen marlin swordfish and dorado — species that were legally reserved for sport fishermen. Since that time, there have been at least a half-dozen more incidents involving Japanese and Korean long-liners that reel in fifty miles of baited hooks each night.

Cabo Falso, just northwest of Cabo San Lucas on the Pacific coast.

Old lighthouse, Cabo Falso.

These ships often have permits, issued illegally, to fish these closed waters. In February of 1988, the Group of 100, Latin America's most influential conservation organization, wrote an open letter to Mexico's new president, accusing the Department of Fisheries of corruption, of allowing Japanese-owned "pirate" vessels to plunder at will, and of taking up to a quarter million dollars per ship as payoffs to Mexican fisheries officials and police. President Salinas vowed a crackdown, though for the Japanese long-liners it remained business as usual.

Shortly after the letter was released to the press, the Mexican Coast Guard seized the Japanese long-liner *Compremaro V*, fishing in closed waters off Cabo San Lucas, with the usual frozen catch: many tons of marlin, thirty-six tons of sailfish, two tons of snook and tuna, two tons of shark fin (it is illegal to mutilate any fish just to get fins), and seventeen tons of unidentifiable species. Cabo's fishermen were understandably pleased until the *Compremaro V* slipped away in the dark, released by the harbor captain and local fisheries officials. A month later, the same ship was captured again in Ensenada. This time one hundred ninety-five tons of marlin were confiscated and a stiff fine assessed. Long-line permits to twenty-three other Japanese vessels were revoked. But so long as numerous corrupt local officials can issue permits, the slaughter of marlin and other sport fish will continue.

Cabo Falso.

The southernmost
tip of the peninsula,
Cabo San Lucas.

"The great rocks
on the end of
the Peninsula are
almost literary.
They are a fitting
Land's End,
standing against
the sea, the end
of a thousand
miles of peninsula
and mountain."

John Steinbeck

Surf and granite, Cabo San Lucas.

Surf, Cabo Falso.

The solution to the plight of the pargo, snook, *vaquita*, marlin, and totoaba is simple; we are fishing too much and we need to stop. That means all of us: Gringo sport fishermen have to practice catch-and-release fishing; Mexican fishermen have to find an alternative to overharvesting with gill nets and trawlers; the government must find a way to enforce its own laws; and foreign long-lining and drift-netting must stop.

Turning things around is, of course, more difficult than it sounds. If those of us who want to help could find an unobtrusive way to encourage Mexico to enforce many positive laws designed to protect marine life and at the same time find alternative income for the average Mexican fisherman, we would have a good start. There are destructive and wasteful fishing methods; the Japanese are building bottom-dragging nets for scallops, which, reportedly, severely damage the bottom habitats, and the Mexican shrimp fleet (some thousand boats in the gulf) takes everything in its nets — juvenile totoaba, *vaquita*, and innumerable *escama* or "trash fish," some ten pounds for every pound of shrimp, which they shovel off the deck dead back into the sea. Outside fishing pressure — foreign factory ships — is more complicated. The big vessels long-lining, drift-netting, or out for squid invariably are from Japan, Korea, or Taiwan. Most of the alleged violations of Mexican waters involve Japanese ships, and enough of these allegations have been documented to take these horror stories

seriously. Something is wrong here that merits examination, not to indict or defend but to abolish this rape of the natural world. Within Shinto and Buddhist thinking death itself may be transitory, lacking the finality we of the West attach to it. We may come back as a dolphin; the dolphin may return as us. But this unrestrained slaughter is more about money than religion. Criticism of Japan's callous treatment of the world's oceans and rain forests is restrained less because of fears of appearing xenophobic and racist than because America doesn't want to lose out on the cellular telephone markets. It's true these folk have a lot of money. The Japanese people have sustained a remarkably perceptive culture for centuries; they are good stewards of the natural resources of their own country, maintaining an impressive sensitivity toward art, religion, landscaping, cuisine — why not their children's future? They are not only stealing from their children's children; they are depriving all of a rightful heritage, a chance to sustain life — including that of our own species — on earth. In this arena of Baja's unpolluted oceans, only extinction is irreversible. Pressure must be brought to bear. I have my share of stuff Japanese, Korean, and Taiwanese. It will not be easy to rid myself of everything. But I am willing to try. What is clear is that the fishery — the web of marine resources — is on the decline and needs to recover. For that to happen, we humans must collectively back off, a tactic seldom practiced in our modern industrial world.

Sculptured granite, Cabo Falso.

An ex-miner from the old mining town of
El Triunfo south of La Paz. El Triunfo was once the
largest town in southern Baja.

Store, Miraflores, south of La Paz.

Concrete cardon shrine north of La Paz.

Saving things in Mexico has always presented a problem to outsiders. The last wolves and perhaps grizzlies exist in Mexico because the ranchers who own entire mountain ranges are rich enough to lose a few cows to predators without retribution. "The worst thing you can do," says a friend who fights to save sea turtles, "is turn something over to a Mexican bureaucracy." Democratic process and equal economic opportunity seem at odds with preserving natural resources. After all, most of the Third World only wants what we have enjoyed for a long time.

There is no romance in the poverty of the northern cities. Most of lower Baja, however, has a standard of living higher than much of Mexico. My friend Salvador worked several seasons in California only to be drawn back to Magdalena Bay by homesickness — the call of the land he loved. He now makes a decent living as a fisherman and as a whale-watching captain during the winter months. But even with no income he still wanted to live in Puerto López Mateos: "It's very beautiful here," he says, "and it never freezes."

Everywhere there is the problem of too many people, and Mexico's population is growing very rapidly. Development sometimes makes living easier, but easy living draws crowds, which spill out onto a land that cannot comfortably support large populations. The land ends up transformed into something unlivable for all. In Baja, the southern tip — the cape — has seen the most of modern developments, and this lovely and complex region has suffered like no other part of the peninsula from the attentions of the international tourism and resort industries. I have traveled to the bottom of Baja only three times in the last twenty years, as if to escape the paradox the cape region hurls at us. The curl of surf around the toes of raw granite headlands, the runoff, the rills back down the blinding white shingle still take the breath away. But it is now nearly impossible to find one of these beaches without the recent spoor of many tire tracks from packs of ATVs.

One hears complaints from tourists of trash and overgrazing. These are valid though minor gripes; it is true that it's hard to find a spot of Baja not overgrazed and it would be interesting to set some areas apart to see the botanical diversity of this land without domestic livestock.

The good news about the Baja Peninsula is the same as it was when the land was ruled by the Giants: this rugged land has its own set of rules and tolerates imports poorly. Most attempts to change the desert into something foreign have failed. The physical lay of the land looks much as it did when the Spaniards arrived; the interior sierras and tableland are largely undisturbed by the presence of industrial man, and there are still a few roadless sections of wild coast.

What to do with this lovely arid land is a strictly human concern whose consequences will have more importance to *Homo sapiens* than to the rest of the natural community. The hand of modern man will pass over the land as a shadow of a cloud passing before the sun. In the short run, decisions will be made about sustained yields, economic progress, and tourism development. Investment money will be solicited and sunk into projects that investors hope will give them back even more money. Portions of worthless land and areas less promising for investment will be proposed for parklands.

It has struck me that the people of Mexico and of the Baja Peninsula have an opportunity that the United States lost sometime earlier in this century: to set aside democratically and inexpensively a magnificent set of biological ecosystems as national parklands. Mexico already has a great start: the Parque Nacional Constitución de 1857, the Sierra San Pedro Mártir Park, the Natural Desierto Central de Baja California, the whale-calving areas of Ojo de Liebre, San Ignacio, and Magdalena Bay, the Archaeological Zone in the central sierras, and the wildlife refuges of the gulf islands.

In the United States, the establishment of national parks is limited not only because of the lack of remaining wildlands — which were largely neglected because of their low potential for turning a buck — but also because there is the notion that these wastelands must be diligently managed in order to remain worthless. Management means the infusion of money; it is unthinkable today to have a national park without building access roads, visitor centers, picnic areas, and campgrounds staffed by well-paid maintenance crews to build and clean up, interpreters to explain what's out there, and park policemen to bust or rescue us when we stray off the path or get lost.

Because of the lack of funds for these mostly unsolicited services, Mexico's national parks are — in my opinion — a superior operation whose potential success is just beginning. The biggest threat to Baja's remaining wildlands is road-building, especially punching through roads that go nowhere, simply to open up the country. The country is already open enough. The greatest need in the park system of Baja is several large hunks of wild coastline: there are roadless candidates north and south of Bahía de los Angeles, between La Paz and Bahía Agua Verde, and several chunks of Pacific coast. These regions could be declared parkland without

spending money. Allowance would be made for the few people who live there, and, other than coloring the map green, the place would be let alone. If a threat to its natural integrity comes along, deal with it then. No new roads, no rangers, no visitor centers, no rescues, no services. Cheap travel and fair opportunity for all.

In a little over a hundred years we have come to a curious juncture. This epoch began with wild Indians, herds of millions of bison, the Colorado River without dams, the endless fertility of the Gulf of California — a native richness that looked as if it would continue forever. Later, resources were clearly declining and conservation efforts were begun. The well-being of the natural world became a barometer for our quality of life. We humans looked to the miner's canary for premonitions of our own doom.

At the end of the twentieth century animal and plant species are reaching extinction at an accelerating rate previously unknown throughout geologic history. At the center of this tempest stands man's unwillingness to see himself as a product of natural evolution. Simply put, that which evolves does not persist without the continuation of those conditions and wild habitats that created it. In our frenzy to track the sign that might show us our destiny, we have become our own canary.

Looking northeast from Cabo Falso toward the Sierra de la Laguna.

photographer's note

I have made numerous trips to Baja over the years beginning with my first trip to Tijuana in 1957. Ever since that time I have had a keen fascination for this magical place. I have traveled throughout the peninsula, most often taking photographs, but sometimes not — sometimes merely taking it all in. Although I began to photograph in Baja in the early 1970s, the majority of the photographs in this book were shot in the last year and a half, from the fall of 1989 to the spring of 1991. My only regret is that I didn't have more time to work on this project, but one could spend a lifetime doing the region justice.

What I have tried to do in this book is to give a feeling for how diverse and interesting Baja California truly is. ¡Baja! is a look at the region without emphasis on its cities and resorts; instead, I have chosen to focus upon the natural scene, on this timeless land and a few of its people.

We need to be extremely sensitive as travelers, to respect this enchanting, fragile country — for each bit of trash left by the road or on the beaches has its effect; each vehicle track off the road leaves its imprint for many, many years. As I write, here in the beautiful cactus "gardens" of the central desert near Cataviña, I see vehicle tracks all over the desert floor. What many people don't realize is that the next generation of cactus and other plant life are terribly threatened by these tracks. It takes years for the baby cactus to become established and they are easily crushed. When you are exploring and reach the end of the road, you should just get out of your car and walk. And remember, we must respect and preserve everything from the thorniest cactus to the rattleless rattlesnake, which all work together to keep this unique ecosystem in balance.

Carefully immerse yourselves in the desert, in its silence and beauty, and your Baja experience will be like no other.

I would like to thank all the kind and helpful people I have met while traveling and working in Baja. I am grateful to all of them for contributing to this project.

Some who have helped in special ways include: Charles Shelton, Bill Bolinger, Dan Budnik, Dan Anderson, Frank Gress, Dan Bieg, Gayle Adler, Nick Yensen, Aida Meling, Tom Pew, Sandy Lanham, Allen Schenck, Carlos Carmona, Les Line, Carol Ann Bassett, Don Moser, Muffin and Tony Burgess, Anita Williams, Ricardo Villaseñor, Judy Becker, Francisco Arámburo, Philip and Ardis Hyde, Jim Hudnall, Lou Bock, and my family, Suzi, Brady, and Morgan. With special thanks to my parents, Lois and Leeland Tenney, for their endless encouragement through the years.

I would also like to acknowledge the support of Joe Graham and Madelaine Cassidy at the Pentax Corporation, Dana Jones of Aquaterra, Inc., Kathy Radley of the Polaroid Foundation, Yvon Chouinard and Patagonia, Joe Wojcich and Tempe Camera, and Landon Crumpton of *The Baja Explorer*.

— Terrence Moore
Cataviña
March 1991

183

Designed by Rick Horton

Composition by Dix Type

Printed and bound by Tien Wah Press